# CONTE

# INTRODUCTION

The idea behind producing this anthology of the earlier years of the PHRG is to bring to the attention of the current and future generation of members of what is now one of the largest and most thriving parts of the Omnibus Society just how it all came about.

There are not that many of us still standing who were involved at the outset and clearly that number will ever decline. Much good, solid research work was promoted and set down in those formative years, some may well get overlooked without what is hoped will be this timely reminder to check out what is now a rich resource in the newly emerging 'UK Bus Archive'.

The following account of the first 25 years of the PHRG is the current Editor's personal take and memories of that period. John Dunabin contributed a similar account of the beginnings in 2002 (OM 443), appearing only a few months before his death. It concluded with words that cannot perhaps be bettered:

*"Broadly speaking, the Group, as distinct from its members acting individually, concerns itself with the overall picture of what operators did in the past and why, while leaving detailed route and vehicle recording to other enthusiast bodies."*

Perhaps we have broadened that somewhat to include vehicular matters where they have a clear bearing on industry history whilst legislative issues clearly have a bearing on the 'why', but in the main the group still eschews the minutiae of vehicle recording and fleet lists whilst route recording remains ably dealt with by other parts of the Society.

# ACKNOWLEDGEMENTS

In completing what ultimately proved a rather extended project, help and encouragement was received from all quarters of our Group but I would particularly acknowledge the assistance of Peter Hale, Alan Lambert, Roger Grimley and Richard Gadsby.

Sourcing of supporting photographs, particularly where the original text had none, proved time consuming but with the help of the various authors coupled with the efforts of Alan Oxley, John Bennett , Bernard Warr, Brian Weedon and others, accomplished eventually. It is hoped that the overall results provide a sufficiently interesting pot-pourri for the reader. (DJB)

# ANTHOLOGY 1985-2010

## Extracts from the first 25 years of Provincial Historical Research

Edited by David J. Bubier

THE OMNIBUS SOCIETY
www.omnibus-society.org

## PROVINCIAL HISTORICAL
## RESEARCH GROUP

*PHRG*

An invitation to look inside...

Published by
THE OMNIBUS SOCIETY
Provincial Historical Research Group

Registered Office
100 Sandwell Street
Walsall
WS1 3EB

Printed by Henry Ling Ltd, The Dorset Press,
Dorchester DT1 1HD

Design and production: Trevor Preece: trevor@trpub.net

ISBN   978-1-909091-20-7

# WHITHER THE PHRG?

*The gestation of the 'Provincial Historical Research Group' – a name adopted almost by default as no one could come up with anything better – was in an unease that had begun to develop amongst those longer term members of the Omnibus Society whose primary interests lay in the historical aspects of the bus industry and who were widely spread across the country. London's road transport history – always a key element from the earliest days of the OS – had long since coalesced into a London Historical Research Group that was seen to function successfully, as it still does, within its specialism.*

The root problem was that by the early 1980s – a decade that was to see momentous change within the then current bus industry – the OS was experiencing a veritable nadir in its fortunes. Declining membership was compounded by lack of preparedness as to how to confront the many challenges that were arising or to address outdated practices that hampered internal organisation. As regards outlets for the fruits of members' researches, the *Omnibus Magazine* published what it could but was badly in need of a facelift, not aided by periods of disruption in both editorial and production, whilst the *'Additional Publications'* scheme was floundering. This last, whereby regular booklets had long been published and distributed to members at very modest subscription rates, had been revamped under a new Editor but, clearly uncosted, was heading towards serious financial implications that were to see it end ignominiously. Such was the impact on OS finances that the very mention of the words "additional publications" was liable to induce an attack of the vapors in Council circles for many years thereafter! A new Chairman (1984) and some new faces on Council begun what proved a long, slow, haul to turn the fortunes of the OS around, but all too often it appeared as if it were a case of lurching from one emerging crisis to another.

It was against this background that thoughts turned to how the diversity that existed amongst the historically minded within the membership might be better catered for. In what was one of the enduring strengths of the OS, many were already in close contact with one another whilst others beavoured away in isolation and it was to bring all of these together with a view to better sharing of information and ensuring that the fruits of research were properly recorded for posterity that gave rise to the PHRG. The idea of forming such a special interest 'group' within the OS is thought to have been floated initally by Stan Denton (ASD), a retired municipal Transport Manager with published work to his credit. However, the baton was quickly taken up by John Dunabin (JED) and it fell to him to be credited with 'founding' the PHRG and being its guiding light for the next eighteen years. Already well known within the OS generally and with much published research to his name, his characteristic, oftimes sardonic, humour and style was well suited to the early development of the embryo group. Peter Hardy (PLH), Roger Warwick (RMW) and the undersigned were also involved in early discussion as to the way forward.

Following these preliminary soundings out and correspondence the plunge was taken and the formal blessing of Council as to the formation of a *'Provincial Historical Research Group'* sought and duly ratified at a Council meeting in March, 1985. That little was really understood as to what it was intending to be all about was demonstrated by an immediate suggestion that this new group be charged with back-dating of the 'Route Recording Records', another headache for Council that had arisen when it was found that all was not as had been assumed with that particular OS icon. A polite refusal was endorsed by all concerned! It could have become the be all and end all.

.Some twenty or so 'expressions of interest' were circulated with *'Newsletter No. 1'* in April 1985, primarily focussed on receiving feedback (detailed and substantial) on what the aims and aspirations of the group should be. Amongst agreed criteria was that PHRG should strive to become known as both authoritative and accurate in its published work but that no 'cut-off' as to time period covered should apply. As an inter-branch group Traffic Areas and boundaries had little revelance and whilst 'outwith of London' coverage was implicit there would inevitably be cross-fertilization and, hopefully, co-operation with LHRG.

Early projects initiated were a register of 'long distance' services prior to 1930, later published, and the start of a 'United' postal circuit that flourished succesfully for many years, was instrumental in a published history and has but recently been revived. An aspiration to create a 'Who Was Who' of figures in the bus industry languishes yet, but ensuring the preservation and development of the 'Master Operators List' created by the then late Cecil Smithies was pursued with success by Arthur Staddon and was to become an important resource within the Library & Archive.

Just what the library & archive of the OS comprised and access thereto had been posed as an early question and coincided with the start of myriad problems with the housing of same that were to exercise all concerned for almost a decade prior to secure relocation to Ironbridge (later Walsall) being achieved. Those trials and tribulations deserve a telling in themselves but this scribe will certainly never forget, whilst chasing down loaned material, receiving a plaintive plea for more time in which to complete researches. That individual had already held those items in his possession for twenty-five years!

During that first year (1985) the *Newsletter*, bi-monthly, initially typed and distributed by JED, became established. Later others (Reg Westgate, Ken Wrigley and Phillip Groves) undertook a few issues apiece whilst photo-copying was likewise undertaken by various members. Posing members queries (mostly answered), sources of information and much else, our N/L started to evolve.The diversity, looking back was quite remarkable. JED had initially envisaged primarily using the time honoured OS 'Postal Circuit' methodology but quickly acknowledged that life was not sufficiently long given the progress of one such packet! Whilst Council had agreed a modest grant towards admin expenses it did not meet distribution costs and for some time pre-paid envelopes were requested and thereafter the small but growing membership paid a contribution directly. It took a number of requests and spurious rejections, such as the N/L not being able to enter the 'Branch Bulletin Scheme', before *PHRG* became an 'add on' to the 1996 Society subscription.

'Meetings' per se had been seen as a problem initially, given such a widely spread membership, however, one was arranged ad hoc at the Guildford PWE that year, on the Friday evening, these becoming, over time, a regular fixture thereof, open to all *OS* members, after being moved to the Sunday evening slot that was otherwise free. Memorable amongst those was hiring a community mini-bus (driven by a member) to visit another member's collection some miles away from Plymouth and the time at Newcastle when JED's audience perceptibly shrank as the thirsty amongst us sloped away to the bar! JED (a teetotaller) eventually capitulated and joined us. Other freestanding meetings took place in venues as diverse as Coventry, Hereford, Bedford, Manchester, York, Bristol, Stafford and Nottingham, even tagging on to the back of an OS AGM in Birmingham. All were reasonably well attended and deemed as providing useful exchanges of information and making contacts, even though locations might mean they were not readily accessible by all.

In retrospect the first ten years of PHRG was a frenetic period and the group still ran on an informal basis. It was certainly now established, had a number of 'discussion papers' to its credit and with its members having contributed a number of articles to the *OM*, although to be fair we would not have wished to be seen as dominating the content thereof with historical material. It was at this juncture (*Newsletter* No. 64, 1996) that a move was made to a word-processed format that allowed for inclusion of some modest articles, wider discussion issues raised, etc. In this evolving format its stature certainly grew and was further augmented when this scribe finally stood aside from editing this aspect a further ten years on (No. 124, 2007) when RMW took over.

As the *PHRG* expanded in numbers, outgrowing in size several of the Branches of the Society and expanding its activities, so the question of the formal organisation of the Group arose. It became somewhat tetchy at times as JED resisted the idea of putting things on the same lines as applied to the geographical branches. Other than that JED was designated 'Secretary' and the undersigned 'Assistant Secretary' there was nothing 'in writing' from the outset. By1999 things had come to a head, partly by the need to relieve JED (who was to remain 'Chairman') of some responsibilities as his health declined. With his approval a note, likewise headed *'Whither the PHRG'*, was inserted in N/L No. 84. Initially RMW was recruited to act as Secretary cum Treasurer whilst this scribe more directly Edited the N/L and arranged a distribution that was co-ordinated for a while with that of the *Osmart* catalogues that many Group members subscribed to. These arrangements were put to the membership at a meeting in Coventry in April, 2000 where Wilf Dodds joined us as Treasurer. A year later we returned to that venue for what was a first `AGM` and thus we, at last, had a committee and (hopefully) the Blessing of the membership to continue to run and develop the Group.

Whilst JED remained the figurehead and absolutely pivotal it was obvious that *anno-Domini* must eventually overtake us. Nonetheless his death in December 2002, albeit in his 86th year, came as a shock. As mentioned in the obituary (N/L 102) the attendance at his committal service was astonishing, members attending from all around the country on what was a Friday the thirteenth – assuredly he would have had some wry remark about that! Arriving early and looking in at the Stockton Heath church one was enabled to alert the verger to this eventuality, he having only put out a handful of hymn books for what he had assumed would be a low key service for an elderly gentleman. The church was packed and later, courtesy of son Christopher, it resembled a convivial OS gathering.

A month or so later one was slightly miffed to hear in conversation that there had been within some elements of OS Council an assumption (hope?) that PHRG would simply fold with the demise of JED. Far from that, the organisational changes had now placed the Group in good shape to progress and that was certainly the intention of all concerned. Derek Giles briefly assumed Chairmanship until Alan Lambert stepped forward to guide us for the next seven years and bring us to our 25th Anniversary. Much more has been achieved since and whilst the Centenary of the Omnibus Society itself will have passed before PHRG reaches its next, golden, milestone of 50 one can at least fervently hope that someone will be able then to update the foregoing account of its origins.

*David J. Bubier*
January, 2018

# PUBLICATIONS

*A brief summary of how publications have been developed within PHRG. Although the number of commercial publishers of transport books appeared to be proliferating in the 1980s, getting the results of the more esoteric research into book/booklet form remained problematical.*

Although the desk-top self-publishing concept was fast approaching and computerisation developing, the old mind-set of it being as cheap to do a print run of thousands as opposed to the few hundreds really required remained. A two pronged approach was eventually decided upon. A loose leaf format for smaller, interim research, projects that could be updated as required was launched on an on-demand basis. Commenced with an index to *OM* articles compiled by our USA based member David J. Simpson and issued to all current Group members in 2000, this 'P' series has continued in various formats, including CD, to this day.

Meanwhile JED and Derek Giles (DSG) conceived the idea of free-standing booklets, to be advertised generally, on the basis of the sales from one then being used for the next, etc. This was administered by DSG separately from the group from 2001 and had reached five titles at the time of his death, the final two quite substantial paper-backs. In his will Derek left a specific legacy to the *PHRG*, a substantial sum, with the implied wish that it be used to further publishing. Following a thorough review, admittedly approached with some initial scepticism, it was found that the digital-printing revolution now provided a methodology of producing relatively short print runs that could be combined with enhanced design features to provide commercially viable titles. Commenced in 2011 with one that DSG had had 'on the stocks', we can regard this on-going venture a success, this current tome being tenth in the series. *(DJB)*

## DETAILS OF ALL *PHRG* PUBLICATIONS, PAST AND PRESENT, ARE TO BE FOUND ON THE OS WEBSITE

# www.omnibus-society.org

# THE OMNIBUS SOCIETY
www.omnibus-society.org

Are you

Interested in

Researching

# ROAD
# PASSENGER
# TRANSPORT
# HISTORY?

We are a specialised

Group offering unique

facilities within an

established and respected

national organisation

## *PHRG*

## *The Provincial Historical Research Group*

# UNEARTHINGS

**Derek Giles was an avid finder of the obscure in the archives and has contributed a number of snippets to amuse us...**

## Class Conscious Coachman

In the 1920s parties of charabanc passengers in some areas acquired a reputation for rowdy or disorderly conduct. In July 1922 it was reported that a North of England operator recorded names and addresses of intending passengers who called at his office. A representative then visited their home and would book them only if they were *'a desirable class of person'*. One wonders who the operator was and how long his business survived this expensive way of obtaining business.

## Mass Transit?

In May, 1926, Mr Brown of Faringdon advertised his Sunday service to Mass at Buckland. The notice concluded `Adults 1/-, Children 3d, Catholics only`. Over the years there have been many services catering for churchgoers which in practice were intended for people attending one church, but this is the only time I have come across one restricting carriage to passengers of a specified denomination.

## Did the Conductor Carry a Tape Measure?

I seem to remember that in the early years of the last century the availability of reduced fares for children on some tramways was determined by the child's height, a mark being made on the car at the appropriate level, to avoid arguments. *(Unlucky then for someone like a boy I knew at school who was deemed 'tall for his age'! – Editor)*

New to me was situation where there were two limits. In 1924 the Barnsley & District Traction Co Ltd carried children under three feet in height free and those between three feet and four foot six- at half-fare inches at half fare with a 2d minimum. Was this a common practice, perhaps in certain areas? Or did it arise because of the Barnsley Company's tramway origins?

It is nice to picture the conductor carrying a tape measure, so that he could correctly charge young passengers. Alas, I fear that the height limits would be enforced only approximately, in much the same way that children showed no enthusiasm to pay adult fares from their fourteenth birthday, the usual limit for reduced fares for many years.

## COPY OF LETTER SENT TO SOUTHDOWN

From the Clerk to the Regional Traffic Commissioner,
Ministry of War Transport.                    4th October 1943
Dear Sir,

### Road Transport Services

On the 23rd September the Minister of Labour and National Service made in the House of Commons a statement (as agreed by the Minister of War Transport) on passenger transport services with particular reference to the need for reducing the time spent in travelling and also to facilitate essential services as much as possible.

In the light of this statement I am directed by the RTC to say that whilst the situation does not permit anything in the nature of a general increase, the need for reducing long waits and queues calls for action. At the same time it is desirable where possible to strengthen services during the day for shopping purposes in order to lighten the burden for the housewife, especially in the rural areas.

It may be practicable to provide some improvements, particularly outside the peak hours, without any increase in the vehicles and crews, but others will need additional staff and may have to wait -until these are available. The possibility of arranging for the hire of vehicles from other regions will be considered, if necessary. Any suggested increase must, of course, be very small in relation to the existing mileage.

The RTC would be glad to have a report as soon as possible setting out the improvements in bus services which you would consider desirable for the objects referred to above. The report should indicate in order of priority:-

1.      the extent to which improved facilities can be introduced at once without waiting for additional vehicles or additional crews, and the mileage necessary on the basis of a percentage of the existing total mileage, and

2.      special cases where services should be strengthened to reduce lengthy waiting tune in queues, but which cannot be achieved without additional crews and possibly additional vehicles. Details of the additions necessary in such instances should be furnished.

Yours faithfully.

*This letter appears to have been sent to all the operators in the South-East area and no doubt the other Regional Commissioners sent out similar letters. This would account for why Hants. & Sussex (and no doubt others) took the opportunity to try and expand their routes in 1944.*

*(Supplied by Alan Lambert)*

# THE BEF TYPE SINGLE DECK MOTOR OMNIBUS
## BY A.S. DENTON

*An early (1987) 'Discussion' paper prepared by Stan Denton following suggestions made at our meeting during the course of the 1987 Presidential Weekend in Newcastle. Produced by Ken Wrigley, (who sadly was knocked down and killed on the way home from an OS meeting in 1993) and modestly circulated amongst Group members at the time, it was endorsed 'e.&.o.e' but little has been said to gainsay what was written at that time.*

Just over sixty years ago there appeared on the roads of this country motor buses fitted with examples of a new and vastly improved type of single-deck body. They were the result of new thinking – and some artistry – applied to bus body design. The basic concepts, continually sophisticated as the years passed, did much to establish the modern single deck bus and undoubtedly contributed to its popularity amongst large numbers of passengers. A successful industry owed a great deal to this quiet development. As a worthwhile phase of development, it would seem fitting to recall the story in the manner in which I came upon it.

I spent my early years in Crewe, Cheshire. Much as I loved the trains so frequently to be seen there, I was too young to be allowed free reign around their local haunts. My mechanical interests had to follow other directions. Passing our house were occasional motor cars and also rare grey Crosville or white Gibson motor buses. A special treat was a ride in one of these, so I was hooked on buses from a very tender age. Family visits to a distant place called Bradford introduced me to electric trams. Ponderous and fascinating as they were, the rare 'trackless' appeared more so, and both seemed much more antiquated and certainly less mobile or versatile than our local Crew buses. It was an impression – even though later somewhat modified – long to be retained.

We moved to South Yorkshire. Notwithstanding the attractions of a newly opened light railway, I could not ignore the presence in increasingly growing numbers of the more mobile motor bus. Those bearing the fleet name of 'Barnsley & District' seemed ubiquitous. They took my eye immediately as, in common with Crosville, they operated many similar Leyland chassis of various types. The bodies fitted on them, however, were entirely different.

The body floor levels of motor bus chassis in those days were high off the ground to clear the rear axle and wheels. The same type chassis were in common use for

A young Stanley noted the wide entrance of the older type of B&D buses.

lorries as well as motor buses and charabancs. The Crosville Leyland – and Daimler – motor buses had bodies mainly of the normal-control type. These had small rear entrance vestibules with access steps and suitable grab rails to assist passengers. At the immediate near side front, an outwards opening door was fitted for emergencies. A few larger Crosville models just appearing had the drivers mounted beside the engine, either in a full fronted body design or to the half cab pattern solid tyres of course were still the order of the day.

The clear panels of the Crosville buses tapered below the waist-line slightly towards floor level as did the lower rear bulkhead, whilst its upper and joining corners were

First of a 'famous' batch. (© OS Photo Archive)

**PHRG**

neatly rounded off to match. Inside were cushioned seats with cane backs. Their external appearance seemed reasonably modern and was enhanced by a smart grey livery. Fleet name and fleet number in red showed prominently on each side of the bus. I later came across this chassis make with similar body types under various other operators.

On similar, normal-control, Leyland chassis, 'Barnsley & District' bus bodies differed considerably. They had an almost box-like appearance with much ornate panelling, some lined in gold, very wide front entrances with high steps and rear emergency doors. Their external appearance was – by contrast almost tram-like, Victorian and certainly antiquated. The very dark maroon livery in use did not improve this. Internally, the cane seating was not very comfortable. Some bigger Leyland with half cabs had much improved cushioned seating and limited 'panelling', updating their style a little. Painting the lower rocker panels in white in some instances as in tramway practice gave a somewhat municipal touch.

From June 1925, however, what appeared to be their first really modern buses joined the (B & D) traction fleet. 20 light weight normal-controlled Leyland 27 chassis, fitted with Ransome, Simms and Jeffries bodies (111 – 130 HE 2322 – 41) and with pneumatic tyres entered service. They were purchased to meet competition – frequently from fast American chassis – and also to be within bridge weight limits on certain routes. Their 20-seat front-entrance bodies on this type of chassis appeared to be much lower loading. Care in design and finish was apparent in the tapering side panels with the elimination of panel-elaboration, the corners and squares of the earlier tram-like box models. Their sleek, well rounded external finish improved even on the Crosville models mentioned earlier. They looked modern, had moquette covered seating and were very sprightly indeed in operation, earning the local soubriquet of 'Whippets'.

These were followed in 1926/27 by the first of many of the famous Leyland Lion forward control type of chassis, initially in the short PLSC1 version. Fitted with modern looking front entrances by Brush (143 – 158 HE 2808 – 23) seating 30 passengers, their external appearance, finish and overall similarity suggested much in common with their 1925 predecessors but on a larger scale. Internal fitments in the saloon, with even better moquette covered seating, reinforced this impression.

Within two years, many more Leyland Lions joined the 'Traction' fleet but of the longer PLSC3 version. Their Brush bodies (168 – 177 HE 3751 – 60: 178 –185 HE 3875 – 82: 186 – 189 HE 3916/66/17/67: 190 – 193 HE 39T9/20/68/18: 194 –197 HE 3921/69 – 71: 198 – 207 HE 3972 – 81) had an even more modern appearance. The tapering side panels were extended much further, lessening the gap between the body bottom and road level. This added to the sleek external finish, even with a wide centre entrance/exit with three deep steps and a three-rail lifeguard fitted below the body line. They looked particularly smart in a new livery of red, yellow waistband and grey window pillars and roof, now adopted in the transition from 'Barnsley & District Traction' to the new 'Yorkshire Traction' image. These new vehicles had moquette covered seating in the front saloon and rexine covered seating in the vestibule and rear saloon for work people with total accommodation for 30 passengers, moulded 'jelly-type' lamps, pneumatic bells and double folding doors across the entrance. The last batch delivered in 1929 (208 – 217 HE 4220/11 –19: 218 – 247 HE 4210: HE 4221 – 49) introduced the first of what I was to recognise eventually as the BEF style of individual bucket-type seating, of which more later.

Visits to family in Derby now introduced me to the growing Trent Motor Traction Company and their fascinating S.O.S. buses. Also apparent in their fleet however were some fast Daimler Chassis but, surprisingly, almost identical to those on the 'Barnsley & District' Leyland 27 buses, although seating more. Then came a further family move to Bradford, Yorkshire, in and around which were to be seen motor buses of the Yorkshire (Woollen District) Electric Tramways Company, amongst many others. A considerable number of the Y.W.D. buses employed Dennis E type Chassis with – mainly – Brush bodies in a dark maroon and white livery very closely akin to that of the old Barnsley & District Company. Of particular interest however, these bodies, although with front entrances, seemed identical to the 1926/7 and the 1928/9 deliveries to the Barnsley & District/Yorkshire Traction fleet. (The Y.W.D. fleet numbers ranged from 36 to 50, with 51-6 having Dodson-built bodies to the same pattern, then from 57 to 84, 89 to 100 and 103 to 106, all with HD registration numbers but not necessarily in consecutive numbered sequence even within the same batch). It seemed these three fleets, Yorkshire Traction, Trent and Yorkshire W.D. Electric Tramways, had something very much in common, two even sharing 'Traction' in their name-style, but what it was, and whether there were other operators so related, was somewhat of a puzzle. There was no OS help available in those early days and limited book information so, in commencing a broader study of the motor bus industry and its many ramifications, I started on a very long haul indeed. The fact that it led, ultimately into OS membership, was something by way of a bonus.

The results of my studies were enlightening indeed but, suffice to say, they showed convincingly that – often in association with the Big Four railway groups – a majority of the many provincial bus activities owed very much indeed to some relationship with one or other of four major transport financial groups. These were the Scottish Motor Traction group, Thomas Tilling Ltd, the (Tilling &) British Automobile Traction

Co Ltd and the British Electric Traction Co. Ltd. It is with the last two in particular that this narrative is concerned more immediately as they produced the B.E.F. story.

Established in its final form in 1896 as the British Electric Traction Co. Ltd, (BET), a main purpose was to develop electric tramways throughout the Country. Soon associated with it was the Brush Electrical Engineering Co. Ltd. It had its origins in the Falcon Engine and Car Works formed in 1865 at Loughborough to build railway and tramway rolling stock. This was to be the role for the BET organisation. Initially they even shared the same chairman, Mr Emile Garcke, with four directors in common. The arrival on the scene of the motor but was recognised as early as 1907 when BET interests formed the British Automobile Development – later Traction Co. Ltd (BAT) to manufacture and also to operate motor buses. The following year the BET/BAT group moved to new headquarters at 88 Kingsway, London. Around the same time, the British Electrical Federation Ltd (BEF) was formed by them. It was later to become the BEF Federation Ltd.

Its main purpose was to act as the servicing and contracts division of the companies then operating the BET/BAT provincial motor bus undertakings. The BET/Brush association had continued into the motor bus era and the latter had built a limited number of complete vehicles. Some already operated in Birmingham – with the newly formed Birmingham & Midland Motor Omnibus Company Ltd – and London. Chassis construction lasted only a limited period however and the Brush motor bus activities were to be concentrated upon supplying bodies. These were to become more and more the products of the BEF's own team of designers and inspectors. They produced the body drawings and supervised the body construction and vehicle finish at the body builders. With the complete Brush motor bus no longer available, the BEF designers had to select new makes of chassis from the open market. They had examined closely the reliable service obtained by the Central Omnibus Company in London who were using Leyland vehicles. This make of chassis was chosen eventually by the BEF team and fitted with single-deck bus and coach bodies of BEF design, the first of many such to follow in succession in their own particular 'house-style'. Built by Brush, they introduced the BEF/Brush combination which was to last for very many years. These vehicles formed the early components of what ultimately were to be the East Kent Road Car Company, (Deal); Yorkshire Traction, (Barnsley); Worcester Electric Traction – later BMMO – (Worcester) and Peterborough Electric Traction – later Eastern Counties (Peterborough).

It is appropriate to give here an extract from a contribution entitled 'Forty Years with the BET – Some Personal Reminiscences of a Bus Engineer' by Arthur Twidle, MIAE, AMInstT, Chief Automobile Engineer, BET Federation Ltd and published in 'Bus and Coach' Magazine, October – November 1946.

'...In regard to technical progress between the wars and the hand we as operators had in it, it must be remembered that we had to develop our services immediately after WW1 with lorry chassis operating on solid tyres. These were, cumbersome in design and heavy in weight. With the average type of body then in vogue, the power-weight ratio was low and sometimes barely adequate to sustain the 12 m.p.h. schedule then allowed. A few years were to elapse before the perfection of the pneumatic tyre was to alter the picture. On the eve of its introduction rumour had it that, if we could produce a bus not exceeding three tons 15cwt unladen, we should be permitted a speed of 30mph. Wyndham Shire, who had commenced to design and build his own vehicles at Birmingham whipped into this idea and produced his celebrated 'S.O.S' vehicle within the target weight, a notable achievement, from scratch. In doing this he gave me the biggest headache I ever had, for more of these lightweight vehicles were needed for other undertakings and I had to find a proprietary chassis which would leave a practical margin of weight for a single-deck body to carry 32 passengers.

No such chassis was available: the nearest to requirements was the Daimler 'CL' chassis, but the wheel base was too short. However, the Daimler company were always helpful and, by the use of a little more aluminium, were able to bring down the weight by a couple of hundred-weights, even after lengthening the chassis. This still left us with about seven hundred-weights on the wrong side, so we decided for the first time to design a body in its entirety at headquarters, which should be based on strictly engineering principles, and not be a mere job of carpentry. By this means we achieved an extremely light structure, weighing just under 18cwt. This, I think, is a world record. Being entirely devoid of frills, the design was too austere to last for long – and, though it carried people during a seven or eight years of life, I for one was very glad when the temporary craze for ultra-lightweight was abandoned. The work done in the development of this light-weight body stimulated our desire to improve the standard of body design. Progress on design of bodies had been dormant for a very long time, and had not progressed beyond the 'egg-box' stage, with all the constructional details and iron-work well in evidence. It seems strange now that well into the nineteen-twenties, double-deck design had not progressed materially beyond horse-bus practice and that, although the horse had been replaced by the motor, the same generic design of body had held sway for about twenty years. We concentrated mainly on single-deck designs for this type was more suited to general provincial operation on account of numerous low bridge obstructions. Our early efforts to achieve improved vehicles seemed, in some cases, to have their effect. In one case, I took the manager of one of our companies to inspect the first batch of twenty of these new vehicles which we were putting through for him. After viewing the exterior with a look of astonishment he went inside, looking at everything in *meticulous detail: he emerged again and stood looking at the bus with an expression of perplexity tinged with annoyance. As he had not uttered a single word during his inspection, I enquired if we had made a mistake or if anything was wrong.*

*"Wrong?" he replied, "The whole job is wrong. I intended to use these in general service on all routes, but they are so much better than the rest of the fleet that if I do everybody will be waiting for the new bus, and it will play hell with our services. Think! If I take this one off, I shall be inundated with abusive letters from old ladies asking what I have done with their new-bus." I left him to sort out this problem for himself.'* (Conclusion of Mr Twidle's extracted contribution).

Such expert evidence had confirmed, albeit somewhat belatedly, my own earlier impressions and researches which had shown that such BEF type bodies had appeared in other fleets. They included those of Northern General Transport Co. Ltd, using AEC chassis (1925 style bodies); Scottish General Transport Co. Ltd with Tilling-Stevens B9A chassis with conventional gearboxes (1925 style bodies); Wrexham & District Tramways/Transport – later Western Transport and Crosville – on Daimler normal control CM type chassis (1925 style bodies) and forward-control Daimler CF6 type chassis (1927/8 style bodies) and the South Wales Transport Co. Ltd employing rare Armstrong-Saurer chassis for hill work (1925 style bodies). The BET 'empire' was far-flung.

It would seem that the 1928 BEF type body as equipped with front entrance with deep well and folding doors and with BEF type individual moquette covered seats of their particular 'bucket' pattern appeared to have shaped the BEF 'house-style' design for at least the next decade as progressively updated. These models had quite low roofs as, internally, only quite small parcel nets were fitted therein. Early examples were four delivered to Yorkshire W.D. Electric Tramways on Leyland Tiger TS1 chassis, two with, bodies built by Weymann (87-8 HD 3139/40) seating 26 and two by Christopher H. Dodson Ltd (101-2 HD 3504/5) seating 28. Externally in a style very similar indeed to these vehicles was the bodywork built on four Leyland Tiger TS1 chassis for the West Yorkshire Road Car Co Ltd in May 1929. Constructed by Charles H. Roe Ltd, also with front entrances having deep well, folding doors and with moquette covered thick-back coach type seats, providing accommodation for 26 passengers (501-4 WW 9018-51). Heavy luggage was accommodated in strong built-in luggage racks extending internally on both sides of the saloon at roof level. This was a new innovation, soon to become almost a standard BEF type body fitment. It was also adopted by Leyland Motors Ltd in their new body style introduced in 1930 for the Tiger and the revised Lion models. Later in 1926 six similar Leyland Tiger/Roe coaches went to the West Yorkshire Road Car Company (508-13

WW 9791-6), of which 510/11 had even more luxurious seating with thicker seat swabs and higher backs. Eight almost similar coaches were supplied to Yorkshire W.D. Electric Tramways in 1930 (161-8 HD 4067-74). All the fourteen late 1929/1930 Roe bodies had been given a neater and more rounded finish at the rear from the roof downwards and whilst owing much to Roe styling, they bore an unmistakable BEF imprint and seemed to be of a composite design, only to be repeated in four similar models delivered to YWD in 1931 (179 HD 1364 180-2 HD 4365-7). These however had inset entrance doors and seating similar to WY 510/1 and were now approaching a true BEF type style.

In logical progression, the 1929 BEF body style was slightly more sophisticated than its immediate predecessor having some limited rounding-off and a more tapering effect in its rear-end styling; the inset entrance door and vestibule was introduced but this style of body was perhaps of an interim nature, and its use did not seem too wide spread. The principle examples I remember were the Yorkshire Traction PLSC3 Lions already mentioned and the batch supplied to Yorkshire W.D. Electric Tramways but on the newer Leyland (super) Lion LT1 chassis with Brush 30 seat bodies. (111-27, HD 3753-69). By the end of 1929, the BEF style had been refined further in anticipation of the 1930 deliveries taking more or less the final form which, with minor amendments, was to last a very lengthy time as the standard BEF body design. The most obvious change, which altered the external appearance quite considerably, was the far higher roof line, rounded off smoothly to just above window top level along the sides and blending into a very-neat and smooth rear end. The higher roof was necessary to allow fitment of the very deep and strong luggage racks along both sides of the saloon above the passengers' heads. It was a neat and sensible answer to a tricky problem as, along with the comfortable seating which the BEF design team had eventually evolved, the vehicle had a multiplicity of roles and many were used accordingly. The BEF design also now standardized upon the inset entrance door and vestibule arrangement, most commonly at the front and overall the final finish was that of a very attractive vehicle indeed.

Internally the finish developed in earlier designs, and particularly on the 1928 models, was repeated in an even more sophisticated manner. In producing their successive styles of bodywork, the BEF teams continued tidying up the saloon and maintained consistent improvements in general neatness, brightness and passenger amenities. Moulded light shades, suitable grab rails and floor coverings and, eventually, internal saloon heaters accorded well with this approach. Particular attention seems to have been given to seating. Square-backed seating in pairs with one colour moquette covering and finish dated from 1926. The bucket-type pattern seat, generally finished in ribbed moquette and first introduces in 1928/9 had a lengthy life, not the least because it was very comfortable for the passenger. In the

OS '1929-1969 Special Commemorative Book', an article by P.M.A. Thomas of the 'Bus & Coach Magazine', an expert technical journalist in his day, featured his comments on the 1930 Commercial Motor Show. Those on seating are particularly relevant as he wrote as follows.

"...Before leaving the subject of seats, special mention should be made of those fitted to the single-deck Brush body – a standard Federation body designed by Mr Arthur Twidle. In appearance there was nothing unusual about these seats, 30 of which were fitted in a body of standard size and coming within the 26ft overall length limit. If one sat in these seats however one at once appreciated the comfort they afforded, particularly in regard to leg and knee room. The explanation is that the angles of seat cushions and seat backs have been calculated very carefully and advantage has been taken of every inch of room. Other designers might well pay more attention to this important matter, for there is no doubt that comfort in a great many coaches could be improved in this way without reducing the number of seats." This says it all perhaps but even so the 'ultimate' in comfortable service bus seating in many quarters was provided by these fitted in bodies on BMMO SOS 'M' type chassis from 1929 onwards. Was there any BEF design influence?

In Yorkshire in particular the BEF body style was now becoming quite familiar. It continued to appear in reasonable numbers and with new (now) BET associated companies. In certain instances nevertheless the development style took an unusual course, very evident in the case of the Yorkshire Traction and the newer East Yorkshire Motor Services. Their first coaches appeared in 1929 using Leyland Tiger TS chassis. The bodies were constructed by Hall, Lewis & Co. Ltd to obvious BEF design and based on the 'interim' 1929 service-body 'shell' mentioned earlier but with smoother, more rounded-off, rear ends. The YTC models (218-253 HE 4250-55) had front entrances with a wide swing door opening outwards. Those for the EYMS had rear inset doors/vestibules (120-125 KH 7911-7919). 126-129 seemingly were never delivered to EY but – on excellent OS sources authority – appear to have been diverted to the Eastern Counties company and, of course, were finished in their vastly attractive dark blue and primrose (including wheels) livery. Luggage was accommodated in lockers below the floor on both sides of the body. Luxury 'armchair' seating for twenty six passengers was standard, with small folding tables inset into seat backs. At least one EYMS vehicle seated only 23 passengers however (125 KH 7919) as it was provided with a toilet room on the near side behind the entrance. They were luxury vehicles within every meaning of the word at the time.

For the following year, 1930, however the extreme change in standards was truly noticeable. Both operators chose similar chassis and entrance positions (YTC – front; 283-8 HE 4725-30. EYMS – rear; 156-8 RH 20U-6). The Brush bodies supplied however were of the standard BEF service-bus type described earlier. The only concession for what were intended to be coaches was more leg room for passengers by the fitment of only 26 BEF style standard moquette covered bucket type seats, whilst saloon heaters were provided. These vehicles nevertheless ran regularly on the long runs to Birmingham and London. Scottish General Transport had similar chassis and bodies – but built by Cowieson – for their Lancashire and Yorkshire workings. Very soon East Midland Motor Services were using similar vehicles – but employing AEC Regal chassis and Brush front entrance bodies with BEF style rexine covered seating – on their Sheffield/London express, so replacing the ex Underwood single-deck Gilford service buses previously used. It seems too that South Wales Transport took similar vehicles, but fitted with coach doors, for their coaching fleet.

For service bus duties Yorkshire Traction also took further similar bodies but seating the standard 30 passengers and mounted on, successively, Leyland LT1 type Lion, Dennis Lancet and Daimler Chassis. Yorkshire W.D. Electric Tramways did the same, favouring the first two types of chassis. New operators to the BET fold favouring the BEF standard bus body included Hebble Motor Services who used Albion Chassis. Further afield, Scottish General Transport and Western Transport both had this identical body type fitted on Tilling-Stevens B10C2 or B10A2 chassis whilst South Wales Transport chose AEC models. So the BEF pattern had been well established and – with some occasional variations on the 'main theme' – was to continue almost until nationalisation many years later.

The BEF standard body 'shell' continued to be regularly adapted for coaching duty but to much more luxurious standards than the 1930 YTC/EYMS examples-described. The 1932 version used by Thames Valley Traction on Leyland Tiger TSI chassis with Brush body work had full coach style seating for 28 passengers and coach type front door. These were used on their Reading/London express coach services. Similar models but with Weymann bodies and 32 or 28 coach type seats and inset front doors/vestibules – finished in the new cream Yorkshire livery – were supplied to both Yorkshire Traction (360-5 HE 5637-12) and Yorkshire W.D. Transport, as YWD had now become (231-2 HD 1677-8), in the same year. The latter also had two of their earlier 1928 Leyland Tiger chassis with Dodson BEF style bodies modernised by the fitment of this new pattern of BEF (coach) type Weymann body, also in the cream livery, about the same time. (101-2 HD 3501-5). Very similar BEF style coach bodies but with 30 seats and rear entrances and of Eastern Counties construction were fitted to the 1932 Leyland Tiger TSI delivered to East Yorkshire (185-90 KH 1793-9).

Three years later, Yorkshire W.D. Transport repeated the process mounting similar BET style Weymann 26-seat coach-pattern bodies on their older 1930 Leyland Tiger chassis (161-6 HD 1067-72). Likewise attractive and using the BEF standard service body 'shell' again but with appropriate coach seating and 'enhancements' were six new Daimler CP6 chassis with Brush 28-seat bodies delivered to the Yorkshire Traction company in 1933: (367-72 HE 5990-5). The following year the same firm received six Leyland Tiger TS6 chassis fitted with coach bodywork seating 28 and to the similar BEF design but built by the Eastern Counties company (462-31 HE 6399-6404). This combination resulted in one of the smartest type of coaches for its time to be seen. East Yorkshire took similar models – and also some of the bus version by Brush seating 30 passengers – and in both instances retaining the inset rear entrance/vestibule arrangement: (259-64 RH 8928-33). Of passing interest too, this latter company reversed the bus-to-coach change of its associates by replacing the Hall, Lewis coach bodies on its 1929 Leyland Tigers with Roe BEF type rear-entrance service bus bodies and used them for service duty for many years after. Having modernised part of their coach fleet with new Weymann bodies in 1935, as mentioned above, Yorkshire W.D. Transport also purchased two completely new but identical vehicles on Leyland Tiger TS7 Chassis (323-4 HD 5603-4).

The BEF type coaching variants appeared to be their swansong in this particular field. From the mid-thirties onwards, many of their associated operating companies tended to favour luxury models for coaching from some of those available from the normal commercial market. This was no reflection upon either the BEF design style or its efforts. Progressive refinements to their standard body design throughout the

A Thames Valley example. Leyland Tiger TS4 type of 1932 as used on the London service, private hire work and advertised excursions. (Paul Lacey collection)

thirties produced service buses which, even when mounted on chassis fitted with diesel engines – which were becoming more and more common even in coaches – offered standards of comfort almost equating to those of a coach. Service buses were used in large numbers on limited stop duty, coastal resort duty at busy times and, not infrequently, on private hire work also by many of the associated operators who recognised both their versatility and the high passenger standards they offered.

Throughout the decade the reasons for this were fairly self-evident. The basic 1930 style of BEF design was excellent enough in itself, commonly following the inset front-entrance door/vestibule and (centre) rear door emergency exit pattern but refinements were introduced successively on this. These featured a lower floor-line and waist-line, also a single lifeguard rail. Transverse seats over wheel arches gave place to staggered single and then forward facing single seats, 'Jelly-mould' saloon lights were modernised. The higher roof line necessary for the fitment of the internal luggage racks was made more rounded and later partially squared externally, so appearing more modern. Attention was given to the more effective positioning of the front destination box by eliminating the roof overhang. Varying shapes were tried on the skirt panels. All in all every effort was made to maintain a practical design which was well finished and neatly rounded off where required and yet had a pleasing, neat and modern appearance. The result was most commendable.

The same attention to detail was given progressively to the interiors, in which the most noticeable change perhaps was in the seating. The hitherto BEF style grey-ribbed moquette upholstery gave way to a flowered pattern. The final seat version from the late thirties onwards extended into the post-war years. This took the form of a straight top and back for the seat, the latter extended somewhat, giving a more rectangular appearance and a miniature form of headrest. Saloon heaters became square rather than circular. Variations in some instances in the emergency door positioning placed it on the offside immediately behind the drivers door. This made possible a single rear window which altered somewhat the rear end appearance but it was a change which appeared to have limited popularity.

The Commercial Motor Show of 5 November 1937 comments as follows: *"The Leyland 32 seater, also on the Roe stand, has a hinged recessed door which opens outwards. An interesting item of the BEF specification of this single-decker is the use of synthetic glass daylight ceiling panels. There are two large panels which add considerably to the natural lighting of the vehicle."* The Brush and BET close financial association ceased in the early thirties. Whilst Brush continued to carry out BEF style body orders, these were extended over a wider field so as to include Eastern Coachworks, Metro-Camel-Weymann, Roe and the English Electric companies amongst well established body builders.

Yorkshire Traction:
enduring modernity.
(© OS Photo
Archive)

The BEF house-style, so long and well established, continued in easily recognisable versions after WW2 and even into the new era of underfloor-engined chassis. The BEF touch was seemingly still evident in the 1950s too, when a number of associated undertakings received modern 'chassisless' coaches using older pre-war chassis components. These coaches were of semi-integral construction to a system developed by J.C. Beadle Ltd of Dartford. The resultant full fronted vehicles were neat, modern and attractive and their finish could be assumed to have derived something from the long BEF house-style.

Three such Beadle 35-seat coaches using Leyland Tiger TS8 components from 1938/9 chassis were built for Yorkshire Traction (971-3 EHE 381-3). Similarly, Yorkshire W.D. Transport had ten such Beadle vehicles constructed (-746-55 HD 9353-62) whilst East Yorkshire used Leyland Titan TD4 components for their ten (558-67 LRH 958-67). East Kent and South Down, amongst others were also Beadle coach users of this special type, with Southdown having a very large fleet indeed of 50 such vehicles incorporating Leyland Tiger TS8 components. Brush body building activities meanwhile had been consolidated into the specialist Brush Coachworks Ltd. In the early fifties however this ceased activities and its BEF-agent role was then continued by the neighbouring Loughborough coach-building firm of Willowbrook.

The appearance of the underfloor-engined chassis was the next major change the BEF design teams had to meet. Some Yorkshire operators purchased the new Leyland Royal Tiger PSU1 type of chassis. The Brush constructed bodies mounted on these were of undoubted BEF parentage and continued in a most readily recognisable form the close BEF style family relationship lasting already over a quarter of a century without the finished vehicles losing modernity in any way. The challenge had been well met. The 42 or 43-seat front-entrance version went to both Yorkshire Traction (903-22 DHE 334-353) and Yorkshire W.D. Transport (693-6 HD 8547-50) whilst East Yorkshire took seven of the rear entrance models (551 etc, LRH 693, etc). Sixteen more similar vehicles went to the latter in 1952 but these had Weymann bodies. Yorkshire Traction took a further six with Roe front-entrance bodies in 1952 (959-64 EHE 160-5) and ten more the following year with Willowbrook bodies (992-1001 EHE 939-948). The impression one retains of these vehicles, notwithstanding their obvious BEF parentage is one of great size and width, as they were to (then) maximum dimensions in length and width with still, seemingly, the BEF favoured high roof line. Change was however now in the air and it appeared in subtle ways, displacing the BEF style almost imperceptibly. This was still quite obvious in the finish of four Leyland Tiger Cub PSUC models with Park Royal 39 seat front-entrance bodies suitable for one-man operation delivered to East Yorkshire in 1957 with a similar vehicle but on Albion Aberdonian chassis which came a year later.

Other Tiger Cubs delivered slightly earlier to this same company however presented a somewhat different picture. The Willowbrook rear-entrance bodies of 14 of their new coaches in 1954 on this type of chassis, along with three identical models delivered to Yorkshire Traction – who also received seven further examples with front entrances in 1955 – were business-like and attractive with both fleets using a similar primrose finish. They did seem under-powered and hard-pressed however when maintaining the extreme distance schedules upon which they appeared constantly to work. Their body style appeared to have few BEF touches but rather some sophisticated modernisation. From them later variations by both Weymann and Willowbrook, usually in combination with the more powerful Leyland Leopard chassis for both service work and coaching duty led on to the BEF associated companies standard Marshall body constructed in large numbers in the late sixties and the seventies. Whilst it may have been there, BEF parentage and certainly their house-style was far from obvious whilst nationalisation of the BET interests in 1968 brought different approaches entirely to the vehicle/body style story in which of course the BEF now had no part to play.

So concludes its story, fittingly remembered, it is hoped, these many years later for the consistent excellence of its work and endeavours in raising to very high standards the single-deck motor bus body and thereby contributing greatly to the success of the road passenger transport industry. Seemingly it chose to lead whilst others perhaps followed and the passengers entered an entirely new and comfortable transport world. Local journeys where possible, perhaps tolerated by necessity, tended to become enjoyable. People started riding the buses for pleasure. Trips of limited extent in slow-moving somewhat uncomfortable charabancs, open to the vagaries of the weather, began to become obsolete. Only those who experienced the vast changes in comfort and style of these times can appreciate them truly and it seems undeniable that the BEF as it was played a great role in bringing them about. My own first long distance road journeys were experienced in the summer of 1929 on day trips from South Yorkshire to both Scarborough and Cleethorpes. They were completed in new four cylinder Leyland Lion service buses with comfortable Brush BEF type bodies of the Yorkshire Traction company with speed and great enjoyment. Their sophisticated six-cylinder Leyland Tiger/Hall Lewis coaches ran as smoothly as any Rolls-Royce and were just as luxurious. A lengthy Barnsley-Derby (and return) trip in an identical coach of associated East Yorkshire ownership certainly underlined this. Over twenty or more years later, journeying on their Filey-Scarborough service, one of their large Leyland Royal Tiger – Brush BEF type 'new-look' under-floor engined vehicles proved both comfortable and modern and a worthy successor to its 1929 counterpart in which I had earlier travelled and a worthy bearer of the same and lengthy BEF house-style image which, seemingly, had still not aged. *(below, one depicted in 1962)*

In the photographic field, G.H.F. Atkins is one of the few who have recognised and recorded with consistency the BEF-design body style, albeit with a leaning towards Yorkshire operators.

**Photo courtesy Bernard Warr.**

Courtesy of Alan Lambert collection.

# ORIGINS & OPERATION OF
# EARLY CONTINENTAL TOURS

## DAVID J. BUBIER

*Very little research has taken place into early (pre-1930) operation of extended tours generally. The only recorded study found has been that by the late E.L. Tavlor and presented as his 1963 Presidential Address (OM 176). Even here he admits that authentic data is hard to find.*

There is no doubt that following the general proliferation of motor vehicles from just one hundred Years ago there were those who shipped their personal transport abroad. However, it is concluded that this remained the exception rather than the rule and confined to the rather well-heeled. The logistical difficulties at the time were considerable and with little equipment or expertise available at the Channel ports. Although quite long distance Journeys and touring were being undertaken within the UK with motor buses, unless contrary evidence emerges I am of the opinion that there was no attempt to take such a vehicle to Continental Europe for a specific service in the pre-1914 period.

The Great War itself lead to the rapid development of facilities for the shipping of vehicles, vast numbers (including many buses) crossing the Channel for active service. The methods employed still involved crane-lift over the ships side, cumbersome by today's ro-ro standards, but the expertise was there.

Immediately on cessation of hostilities there developed a latent demand for tours to the Flanders battlefields. These were underway from early in 1919, initially enterprising ex-soldiers (some still serving!) using ex-military cars available in abundance and meeting clients from the ferries in France. More structured six-day tours using 20-seat Dennis vehicles soon followed. These were run by Chapman & Sons of Eastbourne and London, a firm with pre-war experience of extended touring. This particular market was quite extensive for some years and several operators became involved. W.P. Allen, owner (amongst many others) of London & South Coast M.S. at Folkestone had offices and a garage at Ostend for a period.

By 1921 Chapman's were offering at least three tours each season further afield. These were generally of up to three weeks duration and variously reached Germany, Switzerland, Italy, Spain and (particularly popular) French Riviera. Vienna, Venice, Gibraltar were all considered within viable range at this time. Other operators pioneered regular services to the south of France, notably Motorways (Lyon & Spencer) from 1920, who later reached North Africa and even Moscow.

Cost of one of the Chapman tours embracing most of the sights of Europe was 18 Guineas, mouth-watering now but then a sizeable sum. This almost certainly set the clientele as the professional and middle classes. Given that and that these must have been adventurous, free-spirited individuals, of both sexes, to embark on such tours it seems unlikely that none saw fit to set down their experiences in print, or at least kept a diary that has been handed down. If such an account exists anywhere it certainly deserves to be unearthed and reproduced.

Those who operated these tours must have been resourceful. The initial organisation of hotels, etc., by letter and telegram was no mean feat whilst the drivers must have been exceptional characters. Fuel, spares, etc. all had to be provided for. Given that the vehicles of the time had virtually no luggage capacity, this same being far more bulky at this period for a lengthy holiday (dressing for dinner would probably have been considered mandatory), a hypothesis is made as to the likely modus operandi. It is possible that two vehic1es were always deployed, the second having a van body, This would carry the fuel supply (in cans – very few pumps then), spares and also tranship the luggage between hotels direct ahead of the tour vehicle. It would also serve as a replacement (by means of body swop) in the event of catastrophic failure of the passenger carrier. There are occasional hints that similar arrangements may have been applied to long distance services within the UK at this period although documentation is scarce.

The level of provision of continental tours ex the UK seems to have remained fairly constant during the 1920s. With improved vehicles during the following decade there was some upsurge and a greater number of operators involved. After 1945 touring was slower to re- start, the recently deceased Frank Woodworth leaving us his account of the organisation of the first post-war EK tour in 1950. Coaches still needed to go on board by crane, although a dedicated car carrying ferry had been in existence since 1931. Ramps capable of taking larger vehicles were built at Dover in 1953 and the rest, as they say, is history.

As has been said, documented research into the growth of continental touring has been sparse. These brief notes are to serve as a guide to what may be out there in as yet undiscovered personal accounts or in industry publications. Anything that other Group members may be able to add would be gratefully received.

*With the move to a word-processor format (from N/L 64), albeit still a double-sided A4 sheet, the options for short articles to be included as 'discussion papers' presented itself and this article was the first such (75, Nov/Dec 1997). A number of misnomers are now apparent therein, certainly, but the preceding article was what the Newsletter was intended to be about, posing the questions and, hopefully generating answers. Subsequent information that has come to light over the years is reflected here but it remains an area where detailed documentation remains tantalisingly scarce.*

- The hypothesis that no one had attempted to take a British-based vehicle abroad for a tour prior to World War One stands. The Thomas Cook archives appear to indicate the preferred option as being train-ferry-train to a major tourist destination abroad and use of local charabancs for subsequent touring.

- Despite the obvious logistical difficulties, travel agents (perhaps more so than operators) organised short break 'Battlefield Tours' from all over the country on an almost industrial scale to meet latent demand for those wishing to see 'Flanders Field' where lost relatives had fought, etc. Until 1922 no passports were required for organised parties up to 60 hours duration, which certainly helped, and this was the norm, with Ostend the most favoured port of entry. Stress was often laid about the 'difficulties' where the areas had been 'laid waste' under German occupation. No corresponding situation appears to have applied to those that had remained under British control!

- Chapman & Sons favoured bench charabancs reduced slightly in capacity for continental tours. The photo (p28) from the Alan Lambert collection indicates that they DID have a rear luggage locker plus what looks like a tools/spares box below. The '18 guineas' price in the early 1920s oddly equates almost exactly to what a comparable continental tour would cost today!

- The time factors involved in craning the tour vehicle on-board in the pre-WW2 period often meant that passengers crossed separately and with hotel accommodation, etc, making for an almost twenty-four hour channel crossing.

- As the account of 'Red Line' (OM 423, 1998) recalls, some post-war continental touring did get underway as early as 1946. As with WW1, one can only marvel at the overcoming of the many difficulties surely encountered in both organising and operating such in a still recovering Europe.

# WHO WAS FIRST?

*In a letter to AUTOCAR dated 15 Oct 1900 Mr R.A. Cobb, of the Margate brewing family, made the claim that "two years ago, two or three MMC wagonettes plied between Margate and Westgate with the result that people wrote to the local papers about the 'tremendous noise' and frightful stench' of these wagonettes and the next year they were refused a licence to run".*

If Mr Cobb was really talking about 1898 then this service, if proven, might well vie with the claim of Edinburgh (18th May, 1898) to have seen the first public motor car service in Britain. However, he may well have been thinking in terms of 'season' in which case, writing at the end of that of 1900, we are in fact looking at Spring 1899, a period when many such services sprung up across the country.

The Daimler based wagonettes marketed by Harry Lawson's MMC company, capable of carrying around six were reasonably robust, and just about the only viable vehicle for the early years (1896-1901), the alternative being cumbersome steam powered units. Numerous attempts were made to start such services in diverse places and it is doubtful whether even half of these have ever been identified and recorded. Perhaps the acid test is whether a regular scheduled service was offered because many were in the nature of 'trips' to demonstrate a ride by motor car. Mystery surrounds when the very first attempt to run a public service was made. The 'emancipation' of the motor car, repealing the need to have a pedestrian walk 20 yards in front, arrived too late in 1896 for anything to have been considered. However, the necessary vehicles must have started to become available during 1897, so why was it not until 1898 and 1899 that entrepreneurs got under way? Perhaps

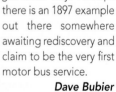

there is an 1897 example out there somewhere awaiting rediscovery and claim to be the very first motor bus service.

**Dave Bubier**

An example at New Brighton.

# ROAD BLOCK – A 1916 ACT

## PETER HALE

*We all know that early motor bus operators had to contend with poor roads. But it may not be well known that in an attempt to address this matter, legislation was passed during the First World War which checked the growth of the bus industry for a number of years.*

Most roads 100 years ago were not built to take the weight of heavy motor vehicles, so while motor buses were seen to be a good thing on the whole, Councils soon found that they damaged roads. Moreover, as there was no road use tax such as there is today bus operators did not contribute anything towards the upkeep of the roads that they used. Local authorities bore the full cost of maintenance and repairs, so it was no wonder that they resented bus operators making profits at their expense.

The feeling at the time was that, sooner or later, some kind of limitation of use would be imposed, so there was some jockeying for position between bus operators and local authorities. Midland Red, for example, routinely sought approval from local authorities for bus services to start, even where councils had no powers to licence them. BMMO presumably hoped that if councils had approved bus services, it would not be possible to stop them or impose a road charge at a later stage. Local authorities, needless to say, were wise to this. When, in 1915, the Mid- land Motor Bus Company (MMBC) of Northampton asked Rugby UDC to be allowed to park up a bus in the town twice a day, the council decided not to actually grant permission, but also not to object to a specified stretch of road being used for this purpose. The bus service started but the council did not prejudice its chances of imposing a road use charge in the future.

The long-expected law appeared in May 1916, in the form of the Local Government (Emergency Provisions) Act. This new legislation covered a wide range of subjects, from payments made to local government officers in military service to the calculation of amounts payable to pauper lunatics *(yes – there is a link between buses and insanity in law!)*, but one part of it specifically affected bus services.

Section 20 of the Act provided that an omnibus could only operate on any route if the consent of the highway authority responsible for maintaining any road used had been given, unless the road had been regularly served in the two years prior to 1 March 1916. Moreover, highway authorities could give their consent as they saw fit. The law did not specifically mention road use charges, but it was clearly' now legal to impose them as a condition of allowing new bus services to start. According to a commentary about the law in the 1919 *MTYB* Section 20 was drafted with charging in mind.

There was a right or appeal against local authority decisions. If the Local Government Board considered that highway authority approval had been unreasonably withheld, a bus service could be operated without it. Consent was also not required in any cases where the Admiralty, Army Council or Minister of Munitions considered that a route was necessary for munitions workers or other persons engaged on war service. From August 1919 appeals were heard by the then newly created Ministry of Transport.

In what apparently was a landmark decision, in 1920 the Ministry of Transport rejected an appeal by united Automobile against the imposition of a 2d per mile toll by three Councils in its territory when granting permission to run 'extensive' services in their areas. The Ministry decided that the charge was reasonable.

Apart from the charging aspect, one effect of Section 20 was to give to councils large and small the power to decide whether or not a bus service in a new territory could start. On the face of it, councils now had the upper hand, but in reality this was not necessarily so. In Northamptonshire, Crick RDC found itself in a dilemma that it had probably not anticipated.

### '... it does not appear that Section 20 was a good piece of legislation.'

The MMBC service from Northampton to Rugby mentioned above started during November 1915. Soon after 1 March 1916 the route was specifically amended to include the Village of Kilsby, which was in Crick Rural District. So, while the original route was not affected by Section 20, the Kilsby deviation was.

Initially the council decided to only let the Kilsby deviation continue If MMBC was prepared to contribute towards the upkeep of the roads it used. The company responded by saying that *"if there was any question of our being penalised to the slightest extent the company would prefer to withdraw the service, as the only consideration for its use had been the conveyance of the public and munitions workers."* Soon afterwards it turned the screw further and actually withdrew the service.

This made the council change its mind – it knew that the withdrawal had caused inconvenience, and that one man had ceased working on munitions as he could no longer get to Rugby. After Councillors had declared that these were *'very peculiar times'* they decided to allow MMBC to run two buses a day until further notice. However, this was to no avail, because as far as is known the service was never reinstated.

Originally, Section 20 was to apply only until one year after the end of the war, but the period of application was extended to August 1921 by Section 12 of the Ministry of Transport Act 1919. This made expansion after the war difficult for those companies not prepared to pay for the upkeep of roads, but ways could sometimes be found. Two which Midland Red used were a profit-sharing agreement (in Nuneaton, in return for exclusive operating rights), or using someone else's route.

The latter occurred when BMMO decided to run from Coventry to Rugby in 1920. The company had reached Rugby once before, in 1916, in response to an MMBC service between the two towns over a different route. MMBC had started in February and so was not affected by Section 20, but BMMO only began in mid-March, in the event, MMBC ceased running its service before Midland Red was forced to withdraw. However, BMMO was later to be grateful for the competition for the 1920 service used the old MMBC route!

By this time, the end of 'Section 20' was nigh, as it was superseded by the Finance Act 1920. This came into Effect on 1 January 1921 and, in a change of direction, brought about the system of vehicle road tax that is still in force today.

It may seem surprising that vehicle taxation was not introduced sooner. Perhaps, as nowadays, the prospect of introducing a new tax was unattractive until the effects of war made the situation untenable. With the benefit of hindsight, it does not appear that Section 20 was a good piece of law. It prevented new bus services from starting, yet it did not outlaw competition on existing routes, even If in reality petrol was hard to come by. Also, the definition of the word 'omnibus' seemed to be too wide as it included: *'every charabanc, waggonette, brake, stage coach or other carriage plying for hire or used to carry passengers at separate fares.'*

A horse-bus service was enough to make a road exempt from Section 20, so long as it had operated regularly at any time during the two years before 1 March 1916!

Section 20 clearly did have a considerable effect on the growth of the bus industry for a few years. One vital question to keep asking when pondering over research notes is *'Why did that happen?'* For the WW1 period, Section 20 of the Local Government (Emergency Provisions) Act can possibly provide some of the answers.

# THE 1916 'EMERGENCY POWERS' ACT – THE FEEDBACK

*We were gently chided by several senior members for almost implying that we had 'discovered' the 1916 Act whereas the 'Bell Street' authors of 'East Surrey' (Reg Durrant, John King & George Robbins) had provided a sound commentary on its effects as long ago as 1974. Nonetheless it was a timely reminder of its importance and useful supplementary information was soon added.*

JED opined that buses were seen as being for 'frivolous' use but that rather ignores evidence of the value placed on their conveying essential workers and for recreational journeys from army camps. He does, however, rightly identify that operators paid some specific taxes (below) that were not then (or indeed subsequently) directed to adequately reimbursing local authorities. Peter Jaques doubted whether conserving petrol supplies was so much a factor as the need to limit the need for labour and materials for road maintenance, a fact made clear some nine years later in a Departmental Report on PSV licensing. John Hibbs considered the 1916 Act as a contributory factor in the formation of the East Kent Road Car Co, where Tilling, BAT and independent interests were merged to better negotiate with a myriad of conflicting local authorities, partially true perhaps. Arthur Staddon pointed out that the requisitioning process had left a severe shortage of vehicles, such that wholesale expansion was not really on the cards anyway.

The real lesson, however, is not to conclude an intentional 'outrageous' imposition on the evolving motor bus industry but look at it from the contrary point of view. The motor omnibus was certainly not universally welcomed in the Edwardian period, particularly in London and the major conurbations where it was seen as both polluting *(More so than horse emissions?)* and as a danger. More acceptable in rural areas perhaps, but most certainly a cause of increased damage (as were cars) to water-bound MacAdam road surfaces. Widespread tarring of such surfaces outside of urban areas was still in its early stages pre WW1. The case for the local authorities was outlined at the time by the prominent social economists Sidney & Beatrice Webb *(English Local Government, Vol V)* and their words (opposite) bear repeating as probably representing the more considered official view:

"...before motor omnibuses became popular, waterbound granite macadam or flint could be used to keep roads in good condition, but now had to be strengthened and surfaced with bituminously bound material at twice the cost. Anyone travelling over roads that have not recently been specially surfaced can tell at once that they are passing over a 'bus route' by the waviness, corrugations and deep holes!" Report by H.T. Chapman, Kent CC Surveyor, 1914.

# THE CONTRARY VIEW

**Sydney & Beatrice Webb at work.**

'What today – 1913 – is bringing the matter to a head is the rapid multiplication of the motor omnibuses, which have been almost suddenly introduced to our roads, chiefly in and around London. These latest of the 'new users of the roads' are proving terribly destructive, not only to life and limb, but also to road surfaces. During the year 1912 the 2,500 motor omnibuses killed a foot-passenger in the London streets every other day! Such ponderous conveyances, weighing, when loaded, between six and seven tons each and travelling at the rate of ten or twelve miles an hour, charge down suburban roads with a momentum for which the road administrators have made no adequate preparation. These motor omnibuses now contribute largely, in licences and petrol tax, towards the Road Fund; but the Local Authorities, whose highways they are destroying, receive no aid from this fund towards the heavy burden thrown on ratepayers. The Local Authorities are slow to move, and backward in discerning what to ask for. But the pressure that they can exercise, coupled with the justice of their case, will, in our judgement, soon compel the Government to redress their grievances.' And it came to pass...

The Thames Weald heyday included 'big-bus' operation in the form of this Bedford VAS (UK Bus Archive).

Ford G299 PKN depicted in Romford in 1993 (courtesy P.R. Wallis).

# DR H. NESBITT HEFFERNAN, MBE, PROPRIETOR OF THAMES WEALD LTD

*Often it is the case that the business of an operator can become well known but the person behind it remain an enigma. Fortunately David Harman conducted an interview with Dr H.N. Heffernan that provides an insight. (N/L 96, Sept/Oct 2001)*

H. Nesbitt Heffernan's early life was spent in India where his father was in the Indian Army. (I am not sure whether he was actually born in India) *[he was, 1913 in Madras –ed]*. In due course he was sent to boarding school in England; during the holidays staying with a maiden aunt who lived at Canford Cliffs – near Bournemouth. It was here that his interest in the motor bus was first awoken. The maiden aunt was something of a notable local personage; in the summer, charabancs would pause briefly outside her house, whilst the driver or guide would announce through a megaphone *'this is the residence of Miss ....... '* followed by a brief account of her good works in the town. The many charabancs in their varied colours fascinated the young Heffernan; as he watched from his bedroom window and he took to going down to the town to observe their comings and goings and those of the local buses too. The only ones he could recall were Royal Blue (Elliott Bras) and Hants & Dorset. He soon resolved that the omnibus business was to be his chosen career and, with school days soon to end, wrote to various firms seeking employment. He thought Hants & Dorset was too small, but its larger neighbour to the east, Southdown, seemed an attractive proposition and there were other, including companies in the north-east (names he could not recall). The letters brought encouraging replies. However all this was to no avail, as news of his aspirations had meanwhile filtered back to India. His parents, like Queen Victoria, were far from amused, They had already decided that he was suited to a medical career, on the somewhat unscientific premise that he had 'delicate hands'. So, rather than the hurly-burly of pre-Road Traffic Act bus operation his future was destined to be Cambridge medical school and the routine life of a GP. There was no question of debating the issue. As he wistfully told me, *"In those days, one obeyed one's parents wishes".*

Come WW2 and Dr H served in the Royal Army Medical Corps being posted, perhaps not entirely by accident to India. In his service, he encountered many cases of shell-shock, a condition then little better understood than it had been in WW1. The diagnosis and treatment of this became his specialisation. The end of the war, demobilisation and the later formation of the NHS, saw Dr H. move from general practice to hospital consultancy. His interest and expertise in treating shell-shock and related mental illnesses were rare ones. These were days of un-enlightened attitudes, typified by the 'asylum' system, with the mentally ill simply locked away;

out of sight, out of mind. Psychiatry was an unfashionable medical backwater. He obtained a post at Darenth Park Hospital in Dartford (South East Thames Regional Heath Authority) with ease and duly progressed to become consultant psychiatrist there. By the late 1950s/early 1960s however the demands of the job were such that he was in a position where, as he delicately put it *"one had the opportunity to pursue other interests"*. Gradual cutbacks in local bus services and their consequent effect on the mobility of those in the locality without cars led him to recall his youthful ambition. Hence, the Thames Weald Travel Society (later to become Thames Weald Ltd) was born, initially to run a Sevenoaks-Gravesend route. The development of the company and its routes are covered elsewhere. **(There are many references in the Transport Ticket Society Journal, also OM 164 and 324, London Bus Magazine 41, etc)**

Dr H did not recount the details but there are some other points of interest from what he said:

- The Dartford Tunnel was, of course, the catalyst, along with the unsuccessful attempts by LT to run bus services through it. When the tunnel opened on 18 November, 1963, LT put on the 300 (later 399) route linking Dartford with Grays and soon disappointed to find that Dartford folk had no pressing desire to visit Grays and neither were Grays Folk clamouring to visit Dartford! Hardly surprising, the two communities, hitherto completely isolated from one another by the Thames, might just as well have been a thousand miles apart. The 399 limped on until 1967. A Green Line 122 route from Dartford, through the Tunnel and up the A11 to Aldgate was equally fruitless. Then there was the peculiar 'Tunnel cycle bus' run by LT on behalf of the Dartford Tunnel Joint Committee which patiently awaited the squadrons of cyclists who mysteriously never materialised. However, Dr H knew that what local villagers most wanted was access to good shopping facilities. One day he drove Essex to have a look around and decided that Romford with its extensive shops and large open-air market fitted the bill. He then applied for a licence for a route carefully designed to avoid treading on LT or Eastern National's toes.
- The livery (lilac or lavender blue), he said this was chosen because it was the colour used by the Royal Blue charabancs. At the time of the interview this seemed to me strange. Surely Royal Blue coaches were painted ... royal blue? However; the recent Ian Allan pictorial book 'Glory Days: Royal Blue' does confirm that the original livery was in fact a light lilac-blue. *[One reference gives Thames Weald as 'Cornflower Blue' – ed]*. The last set of tickets went up 10 £6 in value. The higher values were all ordered for the post-deregulation service to Crawley. This route required a driver to be employed, at the Crawley end, where one of the buses was out-stationed. On one occasion, when the bus returned to West Kingsdown for servicing, a Chessington World of Adventures

sticker was noted in the windscreen. He then came to the tentative assumption (later proven) that the driver was using the bus for unauthorised private hires. That led to the end of the Crawley service. The tickets came in useful on the other services as inflation gradually pushed fares up. However at the end, the maximum fare of £7 just exceeded the highest value.

- The end. Dr H claimed that he had to close down as he could no longer afford to run. The Council was, in effect, unfairly competing with him by using Social. Services mini-buses to ferry people to and from the towns. They had poached his customers. He never believed in, nor had ever sought, subsidies. There certainly was Council competition; whether this was the main reason for the decline in patronage can be questioned. OS member, Robin Pallet, told me that Dr H's night vision had deteriorated to the extent that passengers felt unsafe when he was driving, and hence deserted the service. As the main route involved negotiating the maelstrom of traffic on the M25, anxiety on the part of passengers over being piloted by an 80 plus year-old driver was probably justified. It is suspected that the first announcement (in 1997) that the services would cease may have been because Dr H had by then difficulties renewing his annual driving licence. Perhaps that convinced him that renewing it in 1998 would be even more difficult and therefore that 1998 had to be the final year. He employed just one other driver (other than the Crawley fellow) for many years, a slightly younger lady [nb: actually his wife, Ilse, who died in 1997 – ed]. All maintenance work on the minibuses was done by a local garage.
- Thames. Weald always used punch-tickets; the first set were geographical, and had more than a passing resemblance to H&D's first type. Whether Dr H actually remembered these is a matter for conjecture. Numerical stage tickets had come in from 1924, but the geographicals may have lingered on beyond that as stocks were used-up.
- The bus services ceased on 28 March without replacement. The Solefield School service passed to West Kingsdown Coaches. His death took place on 6 November, 2000 and was announced in the Sevenoaks Chronicle on the 9th.

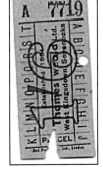

Having lived in Brentwood/Shenfield and subsequently near the other end of the route in Tunbridge Wells I knew the Thames Weald service quite well, travelling on it several times. I often saw Dr H wearing his trademark beret, parked in the lay-by at Romford Market Place, quietly eating his sandwiches, or steering the little Transit sedately along the M25 at 40mph, with streams of traffic hurtling by in the fast lanes. Although he had a reputation form being brusque, I always found him courteous, albeit somewhat reserved. If you, as I routinely did, asked him for a set of tickets, he would carefully tear-off one of each value from the rack and pass them over with barely a word. He was a busman but was not by any stretch of the imagination a bus enthusiast. Thames Weald was a business (but one he increasingly had to subsidise) and when I saw him just after the final day he was not in the slightest bit sentimental about it ceasing. The tax discs had already been sent away to obtain a refund; the destination blinds and DART tags had been removed from the minibuses. The buses had already been sold (to T.J. Walsh of Halifax). He was busy clearing up the-paperwork. I think he had a son, but it was his daughter of whom he was especially proud – she was a senior diplomat with the British Embassy in Beijing and he was looking forward to having the time, at long last, to fly out to China to see her. One cannot help wondering whether he might have become one of the great bus pioneers – if only he had disobeyed his parents' wishes!

# IS THIS AN (UNENVIABLE) RECORD?

In the Autumn of 1933, Mr R.W. Toop, who was later to become one of the partners in Bere Regis & District, was in trouble with the Southern Traffic Commissioners, who suspended his Poole–Bere Regis service for a fortnight. Hants & Dorset had submitted that he was not a fit and proper person to hold a road service licence on the following grounds:

'That Mr Toop uses unlicensed vehicles, unlicensed drivers, operates over unlicensed routes, operates at unlicensed times, operates services he is not licensed to run, does not run at the scheduled times, cuts fares, does not issue tickets, hires vehicles without notice of them being hired, runs without conductors, takes short cuts, runs coaches without destination marked or with wrong destination marked, uses all his buses for private contract work when they ought to be used on the service, and uses unlicensed motor cars to go round collecting passengers.'

The Chairman warned Mr Toop that in future the only course open to the Commissioners would be to revoke and not suspend his licence. (submitted by Derek Giles)

PHRG member Andrew Waller was later (2012) to publish his book 'Bere Regis & District, Life & Times of Country Busmen' that expands on this episode.

# LANCASHIRE UNITED – A CASE OF ARRESTED DEVELOPMENT

*JED's first medium size article appeared in N/L 90. Hitherto, although obviously containing a high content of his queries and observations on others, his longer pieces had gone to the OM almost as a matter of policy in order to keep our name forward there.*

From the late 1920s to the middle 1930s the regional bus companies, to some extent on their own initiatives but also as a result of wholesale purchases, acquired a major stake in middle and long distance express services, excluding peak summer holiday excursion type operations. There were big variations however between them, and one can perhaps see patterns emerging. Medium to large independents took little part in this move, and neither in general did many with recognisable tramway ancestry, such as Devon General, Midland General, PMT, Rhondda and South Wales Transport. Lancashire United and West Riding (with, incidentally, some informal links) fell into both categories and the GM of the latter stated publicly his view that bus companies should stay out of this field. The case of Lancashire United is one of the most striking. With a quasi-monopoly of a densely populated area – its municipal partners were largely barred from this activity – its performance was lack-lustre, markedly so by comparison with its younger northern neighbour. At the 1931 deadline its independent operations were confined to a handful of once daily summer services to Blackpool, with no intermediate fares, which meant that the only towns in Lancashire south of the Ribble with no facilities to and from Preston (and consequently for the Lake District and Scotland) were those LUT served exclusively.

Its share of one of the most intensive of the country's express services, that from Manchester to Blackpool was derisory, even though several journeys deviated via Walkden and Westhoughton, towns firmly in its territory, On what was probably the most important cross country for many years, the limited stop Liverpool – Newcastle, etc, service, LUT only joined in latecomer when full extension west of Manchester occurred. An earlier application under the 1930 Act – an act of desperation?- for Manchester – Glasgow / Edinburgh services stood no chance of success.

Looking back less than a decade however, the picture was very different, TBR Included the local services of most, possibly all major operators of the day, with a great many more also, presumably with equal thoroughness, the much smaller number of 'distance' services. Most of those listed were powered from London, with only a sprinkling not serving the metropolis, mirroring the reality of the situation. One name stands out, that of Lancashire United.

The January 1922 issue contained the names of around 25 'chara' proprietors nationwide, with no others at all in Lancashire. In September of that year LUT was shown as running from Liverpool to Blackpool on Su & W (local operator Collingwood ran D), to Chester on SSu, to Llangollen SuW and to Southport on WO, from Manchester they went to Blackpool D, Llandudno S and Llangollen WS. No mention of services from Liverpool by Collingwood or LUT appeared in the August 1923 edition – an oversight possibly – but the latter company was still shown as running D between Manchester and Blackpool via Eccles, with single and return fares from both ends.

What happened after this adventurous start? Was it a case of burnt fingers, were there major financial problems, or was there just loss of will? As an outsider it always seemed to me that LUT didn't try hard enough, and when they did try they got there too late: I have a memory of a comment in print by the late W.J. Crosland-Taylor about a meeting held in Liverpool to decide on spheres of influence and prevention of overlapping. He attended for Crossville and Major Hickmott no doubt represented Ribble. E.H. Edwardes of LUT had been invited but declined, saying he would come in later. Too late?

But the poor showing of LUT did not stop there. For years the company had nothing which could be described as a motor coach, or even a 'DP' with a good looking exterior to match others on Liverpool – Newcastle. Even in the 1950s its buses on, for example, Manchester – Blackburn (Bolton CT/LUT/ Ribble, ex Cronshaw) had an austere look. When at last the momentous decision was taken the resultant Roe-bodied, exposed bonnet, Guys had a distinctly 'battle tank' look about them. For the Manchester – Blackpool service some much lauded Northern Counties Guy double decks were obtained. The heating system was said to be the last word in its day, but it needed to be; there were no platform doors.

Another aspect was that of enquiry booking offices. In Liverpool, at the limited stop terminus in Mount Pleasant, there was a staffed waiting room, but in later years the terminus moved firstly to a patch of waste ground in Russell Street, then to Canning Place. The pokey kiosk provided there was a disgrace. In the other major towns the company served, Bolton, Wigan, Warrington and Manchester (a moribund agency in the Exchange Hotel here must have been a survival from better days), no enquiry offices at all existed. In the 1960s improvements at the Newton le Willows interchange, one of the busiest out of town such in the country, a brick building to house an LUT timekeeper was provided but manning did not survive for very long. On a related aspect, the company's most important terminus in the great city of Manchester (in Salford actually), was sited in a gloomy cavern covered by railway tracks, with no amenities at all.

But nothing lasts, good or bad. Starting from a very low base, in the last decade of its existence Lancashire United started to change. A very visible alteration was the extensive renovation of the enquiry offices in Atherton and Leigh which on reopening, along with the Farnworth office, offered a full range of services for holiday-makers, possibly outdoing its northern neighbour.

It might have been thought that no gaps remained in the express service network in South Lancashire, but the men at Howe Bridge found quite a number, if only as joint operations and/or weekends. Some were based on the company's entrenched rights on the Liverpool – Warrington – Manchester artery, viz, Liverpool – Nottingham and Liverpool – Skegness and the Initiatives may nave come from their partners but the upsurge was real. The list of 24 'X' services in the 1973 timetable included a number where the LUT interest was purely' nominal, such as those contributed to the East Lancashire pool by Yelloway, but some were quite independent, such as Earlestown – Skegness and Farnworth – Pwllheli (both weekends only), and a Liverpool – Liverpool Airport – Manchester Airport service running twelve times daily.

The most striking development occurred in 1969 when LUT applied for a summer service to Cheltenham, that all powerful magnet, with a final picking up point at Newton interchange which would have put most of South Lancashire into its catchment area. This was lost because of Ribble objections, but the service itself, back extended to start from Rochdale and beyond Cheltenham to Torquay and Paignton, with Yelloway sharing, became a reality. Lancashire United had arrived!

## THE RESPONSES

Bruce Maund and Derek Giles provided detailed responses to the discussion paper put forward by JED in N/L90. Both suggest that the long-time presence at senior level of E.H. Edwardes, (management level from 1901, GM from 1910 and not retiring, as Chairman, until 1955) was a significant factor in the perceived old fashioned attitudes of the firm. He was essentially a tramway manager, as such an engineer and almost by definition having little knowledge of or interest in traffic matters. Vehicles were bought for engineering reasons and comfort would not be a significant factor.

LUT acquired three Dennis charabancs in 1914 that went to the WD and made a second start in 1919 with some forty vehicles purchased over two years. In 1922 an agreement was made with Avery & Roberts who were operators at Criccieth but also motor traders in Liverpool and who had supplied all of LUT's Dennis vehicles. Tourist Hotels were also involved and the three gained control of Bangor Blue Motors.

**Latter day face of LUT coaching. (UK Bus Archive)**

With a depot for 24 vehicles in Liverpool the influence of LUT there was much greater than in later years. By 1923 the post-war charabanc boom was receding and many of the Dennis were re-bodied as buses and the company appears to have decided to concentrate on developing services. Avery & Roberts managed the company's excursion business in Liverpool until they went into liquidation in 1930. The North Wales interests were disposed of, Bangor Blue going to Royal Blue of Llandudno in 1928 and subsequently to Crosville.

*NB: Bruce Maund subsequently submitted a more detailed article on LUT's activities in North Wales, supplement to N/L 125, March/April, 2007.*

LUTs two-twelfths share of the X60/X70 (Ribble had 7 and North Western 3) is considered commensurate with its area and it was lucky to get a share of X9. The company's Liverpool office at 26, Mount Pleasant always had a good stock of timetables and it was the police who insisted on the terminus being moved, all parties agreeing that the Russell Street alternative was most unsatisfactory. LUT can hardly be blamed for spending as little as possible on facilities at a place that was obviously going to be temporary and it was Ribble who campaigned for the move to South John Street or Canning Place that took place in December, 1951.

After the 1939-45 war LUT pooled their Liverpool excursions in a joint licence with Ribble, who managed them. The Bolton E&T licence also became joint and it is believed that Mileage on the Liverpool excursions was to some extent worked off on the Bolton licence to avoid dead mileage from Atherton to Liverpool. Latter day developments in the express field undoubtedly followed new management, the weekend services being an attractive outlet for vehicles not required on service work as the five day week became virtually universal.

John Dunabin further comments that LUT had a high level of customer satisfaction for its bus services, particularly as regards time-keeping. The Newton le Willows interchange, where eleven services converged, depended on near perfection in this respect and rarely failed to deliver. The underlying philosophy may be found in OM of November, 1969 when the LUT Traffic Manager responded to a letter in a previous issue in which the writer had identified what he saw as poor timetabling of services between St Helens and Wigan with which the two municipalities, Ribble and LUT were involved. Removal of this defect would destroy carefully timed connections at Wigan, all provided by Ribble!

"There is a lot to be said for an overall fleet name covering coaches on the national network and therefore we may see a single fleet name and an NBC symbol on these long distance services"

**The foregoing statement made by a NBC spokesman in February, 1970 prompted the BUS & COACH commentator 'Falcon' to remark:**

"I wonder how this might be done? There is considerable goodwill bound up with such coach fleets as those of Royal Blue, Southdown, United, Ribble and Midland Red, to mention a few taken at random. On the other hand the stranger undoubtedly finds the multiplicity of names confusing... A National coach set-up would be universal and thus a symbol could be permanently carried on all NBC subsidiaries coaches. I would not favour a common livery, however, for practical as well as sentimental reasons. Many passengers have enough difficulty in finding their vehicles at big coach stations or sea-side coach parks as things are."

# A SURREAL WORLD?
## (N/L 118/119, 2005/2006)
### AN EXTRAORDINARY DIRECTIVE EMANATING FROM GOVERNMENT IN 1948

*Roger Warwick unearthed this item in an early post-war Commercial Motor and was wondering whether its implementation was the cause of bodybuilders such as Duple offering reduced specification options from their standard models of this period. This one rather doubts it has always been the practice of coachbuilders to offer alternative levels of build trim around a basic body structure to cater for the differing needs of customers and, indeed, their pockets.*

THE COMMERCIAL MOTOR                                         March 19, 1948.

# A Shock to Coachbuilders

LAST week we were able to refer briefly to an extraordinary circular emanating from the Director of Vehicle Production, which has been sent to coachbuilders. This gives the early date of March 31 as a "dead line" on which the production of what are termed "luxury coaches" is to cease. The document is vague, unsatisfactory and bears an illegible signature. It describes the bodies affected as being those fitted with luxury seats, sliding or half-panelled roofs, clocks, decorative mirrors and other etceteras. What the last-named are intended to include is left to the imagination.

The chief absurdity, however, is to give such an impracticably short notice. Many bodybuilders must, even in these times, be fairly well stocked with materials, parts and accessories for the production of bodies in this class, if class we may call it, but it is typical of the mentality of many of those who, unfortunately, control the destinies of our industry or important sections of it.

With a proper notice allowing an adequate period of grace, the material gathered by the bodybuilders which, in many cases, could not be employed in any other connection, could be gradually used up. It is not fair that they should be called upon to bear the burden of the idle capital thus represented. Apart from this point, arrangements could then be made to modify later bodies so that they conform to whatever utilitarian requirements are to be enforced. In any case, the whole matter needs clarifying.

The phraseology of the circular is loose, and it would be interesting to know exactly what the Ministry of Supply considers to be a "luxury" seat; there is also the point as to what would constitute "other etceteras." These might range from an ashtray to a lavatory. On the other hand, the term might also include something more in relation to the bodywork, such as turtle backs leading to a point, nicely curved sides, or even attractive paintwork.

It is important in this connection to study the position of the operator who will have to be content with some form of peace-time, utility bodywork. If, later, when things become more normal, he wishes to bring his vehicle up to date and to a form competitive with those of other operators, he might easily have to expend, say, £400, in effecting the alterations necessary.

We strongly advise the Director of Vehicle Production to reconsider the whole question, make his requirements more explicit, and allow some latitude as to the date on which they are to take effect.

The modern example of this that springs to mind was Stagecoach concluding the full specification of the Plaxton body was superfluous to their medium distance express operations and negotiating the 'Interurban' model, an option then taken up by others. Perhaps another prime example of governmental inability to grasp realities was when they had to review the items shown as 'extras' on the bodybuilders invoice when deciding what could be allowed under the former 'Bus Grant' for vehicles to be employed (at least in theory) primarily on stage carriage services. The so called 'Bristol Dome' of the 1970s was a no-no, even though it might represent the only destination display, whilst opting to have ash trays replaced by stubbers was likewise frowned upon. One operator who specified bus seats in a Plaxton Supreme in lieu of coach ones had the total estimated cost of the set deducted, even though he would have got 50% had he stuck with the originals! One 'Grant Spec' Duple Dominant was built to a 12m length and passed the criteria, even though the 12m length was prohibited from stage carriage work at that time! Any views as to whether this 1948 directive was implemented in any way would be welcome, but the most likely outcome, like several other things that we have considered in these pages, is that after what were probably very forceful representations the matter was quietly dropped from the agenda. *DJB*

## *RESPONSES: IMPLEMENTATION, THE (FLAWED?) REASONING PLUS ARISING QUERIES AND EXPLANATIONS*

The piece in the last NIL has prompted some very interesting responses which not only give an inkling into the thinking behind that original directive unearthed by Roger Warwick (RW) but provide answers to some other related, contemporary, queries whilst posing some others. Grateful thanks to Roy Marshall (RM), Allan Condie (AC) and Peter Wilks (PW).

RM explains the directive as resulting from representations as to lengthy delays in delivery of new buses against the numbers of new coaches being delivered in far less time. In Nottingham he cites Metro-Cammell being unable to affect reasonably timed delivery after receiving chassis and the resulting hiring in of new coaches from Robin Hood whilst Skills were providing Bedford OWB buses for peak hour duplication. But surely the complaints were based on a largely false premise? The large scale producers of bus bodywork were under pressure due to the excess post-war demand and, in any case, had, by and large, little or no involvement with coach bodywork as such. Luxury coaches were the province of a largely separate sector, one that had mushroomed at this period with many new, small scale, entrants. You could argue that some of these' could have been directed to switch to bus production, indeed some sub-contracting of production did take place around this time, but it would have been a very difficult policy to implement generally, the different expertise required and quality controls probably involving more time delays than that arising from the original complaint.

So, the March 1948 Directive was a somewhat drastic and ill-conceived solution to this perceived problem, but one wonders if those responsible for vehicle production really had any clear insight into the industry as a whole. Quite apart from the practicalities, one wonders whether the year that the Olympics came to London, with it a presumed boost in the incoming tourist market, was quite the right time to deny operators suitable equipment. Clearly strong representations were made, particularly as regards to the point made by *Commercial Motor* as to existing stock of parts, etc, and some compromise achieved. Seemingly, the dictate was implemented, partially, with some rather random interpretations and results.

AC provides a brief survey of 1948 production for some of the main builders. **Alexander** continued with sunshine roofs and trim to previous specification but a noticeable absence was the sweep behind the rear wheel arches, not to be restored until 1950. A token gesture? A batch of PSI for their own fleet also had plywood coach seats. **Brush**, who built very few coach bodies, supplied a last of a style originally supplied to Western SMT for West Bridgford UDC in February, 1948. In March a PSI for the Milton Omnibus of Stoke on Trent was to a more basic BEF design against de-luxe specification normal for this operator from other builders. It seems an implausible time-scale, but had Brush taken heed? With **Burlingham** one wonders whether a number of bodies to bus design would otherwise have been coaches, but there is an anomaly of sunshine roofs fitted to a number of bus bodies in the 1948 period. With **Willowbrook**, who did not have a true coach body in the 1940s, there is no evidence of change to specification for their bus body trimmed to dual-purpose status. Likewise with **Harrington**, **Plaxton** and **Yeates** there is no evidence of any reduction in specification for their 1948 onward production.

Upon one manufacturer, however, the full weight of the directive fell, either imposed or taken very much to heart, that being **Duple**. As RW originally speculated, it is this that was behind some quite major changes in production at the Hendon factory later on in 1948. Cynically, one could wonder if perhaps Duple was the only coachbuilder the DVP were aware of, or mayhap some senior official happened to live up the Edgware Road from the Hyde! Arguably the main coach builder selling on a national scale (bear in mind that many others then remained fairly local or regional for their principal marketplace), Duple were also, unusually, into limited double-deck production in the post-war period. Is there any evidence of delays to those occasioned by giving priority to coaches? If so it might explain why the beady eye of the DVP happened upon them.

PW supplies evidence from the *Vauxhall-Bedford News* for September, 1948, of the end of production for the *'Vista'* body on Bedford OB chassis and replacement by the *'Mk V Service Coach'*. A specific reference to the March directive, this confirms the same body shell as before but omitting the sliding roof, side body flare, illuminated rear panel, clock and internal mirrors. *'Luxury'* seating (high backed) is replaced by the hooped back dual-purpose type. This last is rather interesting, for one has seen both types of seat in Duple bodies dating from throughout the 1946-51 period, unless subsequent operator switches took place there always seem to have been an optional seating specification. Note also that the illustration of the Mk V appears to show *(shock, horror!)* 'Luxury' seating. PW felt sure that the 'Vista' pre Mk V spec was reintroduced during 1949 *(confirmed, it was – Ed)*. The other question was whether any of the Mk V spec models figure amongst the not inconsiderable numbers of Bedford OB in the preservation field and what the production run of the variant was.

## A FURTHER DUPLE DEVELOPMENT IN 1948 – RE-BODYING OF THE OWB

Concurrent with the introduction of the 'Mk V' Duple announced a 30-passenger service bus (the MkIV) was also now in production at a price of £915 (the 'Service coach' cost £1,483). Additionally it was stated that either model could, now that the permission of the MoT had been granted, be used to re-body wartime Bedford 'Utility' OWB at a cost of £940 (Mk IV) or£1,000 (Mk V). Dealers were advised to fully recondition chassis before being sent to Duple and seek written approval of a certifying officer.

Past sources have described the 'relaxing' of restrictions for the OWB late in the war, enabling a slightly less utilitarian bus body to be applied from about 1944, but were some of these in fact 1948 onwards re-bodies? Likewise it has been known for the 'W' to be removed from the chassis classification where the carrying of a 'Vista' style body was considered too late for wartime production. Has the extent to which this re-bodying facility was taken up ever been fully documented? It is known Duple sub-contracted Mulliners, at least, to handle this work.

*ED: More than a decade on from this exercise of revisiting old theories and considering the evidence we were to see the publication of full chassis lists for the Bedford OB/OWB – something once thought of as an impossible dream. Perhaps in some small way we provided a spur to that research.*

**Whilst many of the wartime utility specification bodies on Bedford OWB were replaced early post-war, some operators got a full life from them, with examples still to be seen in the early 1960s, notably Baddeley Brothers of Holmfirth. (photo courtesy John Cockshott Archive).**

Q Stephen Harling queries the reason for the adoption in 1935 by Baddeley Bros of Holmfirth of the Prince of Wales feathers as a crest on their vehicles. His specialist interest lies in the South Kirklees area and he is working with Peter Cardno with a view to publishing some histories.

A common reason for use of the 'plume of feathers' was not so much any Welsh associations but the appropriate motto that accompanied it – the German 'Ich Dien', in other words 'I serve'.

# FURTHER UNEARTHING BY DEREK GILES

*In Newsletter 116 (July/Aug. 2005) he recounts how the Traffic Commissioners, not for the first or last time, displayed a certain lack of grasp as to practicalities.*

Over the years there has been more than one matter in which the Traffic Commissioners have seen fit to involve themselves to a greater extent than legally required. Perhaps the most significant were the lengthy inquiries into an operator's financial affairs which accompanied applications for fare increases in the nineteen-fifties, sixties and seventies.

In 1932, the Commissioners concluded that they should control destination indicators and service numbers. At their meeting on 20 October of that year the Chairman of the Commissioners approved a Memorandum running to 24 paragraphs for submission to the Minister of Transport, a copy of which is in the Society's Library. This Memorandum provided that, unless the Commissioners dispensed with the requirement, every vehicle operating under a Road Service Licence, except excursions & tours, should exhibit the destination at front and rear. Those on express, limited stop, special services and duplicates would be so marked in addition whilst those on excursions and tours would display, for example, 'Excursion', 'Devon Tour', etc., with contract carriage showing 'contract'. Vehicles not in service would be prohibited from displaying destination information. The dimensions of the lettering and thickness of the lines were all specified. All of the foregoing would require additional regulations.

The Commissioners favoured the use of service numbers and claimed that it was clearly desirable that they should control them. They considered three systems. Consecutive numbering throughout the whole country was rejected because it would require five figures for most routes. Consecutive numbering for each Traffic Area, with the area letter added was also rejected because it would not provide for inter-area services. The favoured scheme would require the routes to be divided into three classes. Those within a district would be numbered 1-99 with, if necessary, a second series IR-99R and so on. Other services within a Traffic Area would have numbers from 100 upwards, inter-area routes numbered from 1 upwards with a prefix letter.

The Commissioners said that they appreciated the importance of consultation with operators and manufacturers, but assumed that the Ministry would arrange this. Bearing in mind the criticisms of the 1930 Act in many places, it is not surprising that the Minister and his Department appeared to have no great enthusiasm for further regulations and the subject seems to have been quietly dropped.

# SIR WILLIAM LEVER'S BUS SERVICE

In June 1914 a bus service was inaugurated by Sir William Lever between Birkenhead Corporation's Pre ton tram terminus and the hamlet of Raby via Thornton Hough to provide some form of transport for the residents on the extensive Lever estates in the area. This is recorded in the Motor Transport Year Book Vol.4 for 1919.

There were two buses, a Star and an Alldays and Onions, each seating between 20 and 26 passengers. The registrations of these buses are not traced, but no fewer than 19 Star vans (M1951-69) were registered by liver Brothers, some being later converted to open platform lorries and one wonders if, in fact, one of them received a bus body. Only one Alldays & Onions vehicle (M 3955) has been found in the Cheshire County motor registration records but without details as to type or ownership. The buses used several private roads on the Lever estate. Sir William Lever had offered these roads to Wirral RDC but they had declined to adopt them so the gates were kept locked and the conductors had to unlock and relock each gate as the bus passed through.

The service continued during the war with women drivers and youths as conductors but there is photographic evidence of them also being used to convey workers between New Ferry tram terminus and the Lever factories at Bromborough Port. By 1917 the acute petrol shortage threatened to close the service down and Sir William, (meantime elevated to the peerage as Lord Leverhulme), asked for the RDC's help to get trees cut so that buses could be run on coal gas. This involved the mounting of a large gas bag on the roof. As so many men were in the armed forces, the tenants had difficulty finding the labour and according to the Wirral RDC minutes, the tree lopping was done by Council and Lever Estates men.

The women drivers were trained and buses maintained by Joseph Forsyth of New Ferry, who in 1919 obtained a 14-seater Crossley bus and then tried without success to obtain a licence for a service between New Ferry and Eastham. According to the Motor Transport Year Book the Lever service is said to have ceased some time in 1918 for unknown reasons. One wonders if the Wirral RDC attempted to apply the provisions of the 1916 Act or whether, in fact, the service continued until Crosville introduced their New Ferry-West Kirby service on 24th September 1919 which passed through Thornton Hough and past Thornton Manor. Unfortunately the Lever Estates archives are silent on the whole subject. It would be interesting to learn if any other noblemen were engaged in activities of this kind.    **Bruce Maund**

1.   Motor Transport Year Book Vol. 4 1919
2.   Wirral RDC minutes

# REMINISCENCES OF AN EARLY BUS ENTHUSIAST

Iolo M. Watkin (1910-2004) was one of those pre-war members who rather 'dropped off the radar' in later years although he was known as having a distinguished career with Index Publishers. Contact re-established through PHRG auspices, there were many exchanges of letters between both JED and your Editor. The following was submitted for N/L 82.

"I have recently been in correspondence with Mr Lolo Watkin of Dunstable, formerly of South Wales, an early OS member and a pre-war member of Council. Mr Watkin has written a reminiscent article, focussing principally on London, which it is anticipated will appear in OM during 1999, but his letters have included some additional verbal snapshot views of buses and bus enthusiasm long ago." (JED)

I had the same shyness as you about first joining the OS. Learning about its inauguration and progress from *Motor Transport*, which I used to read in the local public library, I got that same daunting impression, perhaps partly due to Charles E. Lee's insistence on correctness in all things, which doubtless contributed much to giving the Society its great strength. That I did join after a few years was the result of a lucky encounter. Long after the old 'National' Co had ceased running buses in London and built up its provincial empire, it still had a coach business in London, using its former steam bus garage in Shepherds Bush. A newspaper advertisement gave the office for coach hire as an address in Brompton Road, so I went there hoping it would have some of the company's bus timetables for distribution (by the way, the premises turned out to be part of the former entrance to the closed Brompton Road Tube Station). Though opening the front door rang a loud bell, nobody appeared when I went in. On the customer side of the counter was a large rack containing quantities of timetables, not only of National's own areas but also for many other companies. After waiting some time I tried opening and shutting the door again to ring the bell, but still nobody came, so after a further wait I gathered up one of as many different timetables as I could conveniently carry and departed. They can hardly have done much business that way!

Boarding a bus, I sat by a bloke who noticed my bundle of timetables and introduced himself; it was an OS member, Bert Chambers! We exchanged addresses and met again, when he introduced me to his friend Reg Durrant. They persuaded me to go to an OS meeting and that was how I came to join and found everybody extremely friendly. That must have been around 1932. (According to the membership records Iolo Watkin became membership No. 222 –Ed)

Evocative Charles Klapper views of Salisbury Market Day services. It was doubtless in the Roeb⸱

I had only a small taste of recording operators and routes,* but it was enough to make me aware of how demanding such work is. In 1934, while working for a few weeks in the Salisbury district, I was fascinated by the very large number of independents operating into that city from outlying villages near and far, mostly on market days only. I made a list of their names and addresses as shown on their vehicles, most of which were parked all day in a street called The Canal. I was rash enough to show the list to Chas Klapper, who talked me into working it up into a paper, complete with map, for presentation to an OS meeting. Having sought and obtained some advice on research from Chas Lee (who in the early 1920s had compiled the TBR Guide) I thought it would be fairly easy to gather the information, but soon found how wrong I was! I tried to trace routes on a 1" Ordnance Survey map with the aid of Notices & Proceedings, but the outer ends of routes were largely on unclassified roads, which licences could not, of course, identify. I could not travel on the bus in the majority of cases, where the bus only ran into the city in the morning and out at night, which would have stranded me in some remote village in Cranbome Chase or somewhere until next market day! I had no car to follow the

---

* Reference to operator/route recording was prompted by my mention of Cecil Smithies mammoth work. Mr Watkin wrote: "I evidently did not realise how modest Cecil Smithies was about his work of recording bus operators; I thought I knew him, but now realise from your letter that I failed to appreciate his thoroughness and devotion to the work, because he did not make a great show of it or give any idea of how much he was achieving."

...ers concluded Iolo Watkin must be a spy from the Traffic Commissioners! (both UK Bus Archive)

bus and my bike was not fast enough! Why not ask the operators, who mostly drove the bus themselves, to show me on the map over a pint? What a hope! Somebody started a rumour that I was a nark sent to spy on them by the Traffic Commissioners, who were looked upon with suspicion by many small operators in those early days of licensing. Much against the grain, I had to use a certain amount of intelligent (one hoped) guess-work.

*In Mr Watkin's unavoidable absence his paper was delivered to the Society by Eric Osborne on 8 February, 1935, and published in the OM for March of that year.*

Moving to London in 1921, I spent several holidays in the early '20s at Llanfyllin, then in Montgomeryshire, where my father had numerous relatives. Though it was the terminus of a fairly busy railway branch, which would have made it a good railhead, the town was then, to my disgust, not served by a single bus. The nearest I could hear of was 14 miles away at Oswestry (Midland Red and Wrexham & District) or 12 miles away at Welshpool (GWR). On Llanfyllin market days folk came in from outlying villages in what were known locally as 'dixies'; these were very small vans with benches placed lengthways inside. No doubt on other days they were used, without the benches, for every other purpose.

Mention of Midland Red reminds me that my earliest acquaintance with this operator was on holiday at Marden, near Hereford (it was my mother who had numerous relatives there!). I came away with two lasting impressions of MR, who

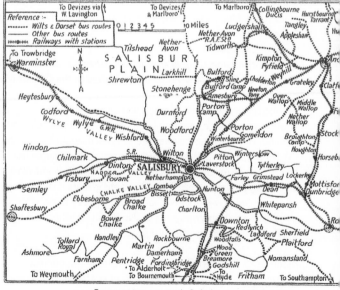

Road Passenger Transport in South Wiltshire. by Iolo Watkin. The Omnibus Magazine, March 1935

Bus routes around Salisbury and Andover

served the village once a week. One was seeing conductors, when not collecting fares, standing perilously on the step to look out for intending passengers (just as was depicted later?) on the front cover of the company's timetable! The other was of a conductor who chose to interpret a company regulation by insisting that, as a half- fare passenger, I must ride standing, in a half empty bus, in case more full fare passengers boarded en route! This was on an outward journey from the city. The word 'jobsworth' had not then been coined, but my mother gave him what she called 'a piece of her mind!'

*The practice of conductors 'riding the step' , was I feel sure linked not only to front entrances but also, if later, to low height chassis. In wartime of course there was often nowhere else for them to go; they acted as a necessary cork in the bottle!The anecdote about the over-officious Midland Red conductor fits perfectly with impressions of this operators staff gained in Hereford a few years later. It must have originated from somewhere high up in the management chain; the phrase 'The Friendly Midland Red' came later. (JED)*

The only other memory of provincial bus interest which comes to mind just now relates to the early years of long distance coach services, as we used to call them. In 1927 or 1928 I travelled from London to Oxford on the 'Rural England' London – Gloucester service, which used the same London terminus (229, Hammersmith Road) and booking agent as the 'Greyhound' pioneer Bristol – London service. The vehicle was very bus like, with solid tyres. I had booked my ticket, as most passengers apparently had, but a passenger got on without a ticket, and – to my surprise – the driver produced a Bell Punch and a rack of bus-type tickets and took the fare! At the time it seemed anomalous that someone who paid on the coach had a ticket to show for it, whilst those who booked beforehand gave up the evidence on boarding, but I suppose that what mattered was a check on the driver's accountability. At Henley on Thames a number of woman laden with shopping got on and the driver came round to them with his Bell Punch before restarting. These all got off at Bix or Nettlebed, but several more got on, paying the driver, at Dorchester on Thames. I don't know what happened after Oxford, but the coach evidently doubled up as a stage service! I think this operator's nose was put out of joint when Black & White started up soon after, using smart looking coaches with pneumatic tyres. However, there was later a joint Rural England and (Red & White)* service, with South Wales connections.

* "The cumbersome (Red & White) title – how was one meant to pronounce it? – was widely used by the companies controlled by J.H. Watts and his associates as a form of corporate identity around 1929, before Red & White Services Ltd was registered." (JED)

# WARTIME PRIVATE HIRE IN LIVERPOOL

*In response to a query whether such was possible during wartime, John Nye provided the following memoir in N/L 110.*

In November 1943, at the age of 16, I began work as a junior clerk with Liverpool Corporation Passenger Transport Department. I was allocated to the Contracts section, which in general dealt with the purchase of all items required to operate and maintain the tram and bus fleet – and was put to work collecting 'clothing coupons' from uniformed staff. However, I decided this had nothing to do with transport, in which industry I wanted to further my career, so I started agitating to get moved to somewhere where I could learn something. As a result, sometime in the autumn of 1944, I was transferred to the enquiry office at headquarters, which section also dealt with private hire.

Private hire in wartime? Yes, Liverpool was a very busy port for troop movements and also these arrivals and departures had to be transported from or to the landing stage or docks to and from the railway stations or transit camps. This happened at any time of the day or night. Buses were generally employed, but trams were also used – these of course caused hold-ups for the regular service, especially when some 800 troops had to be moved at once. Other hires might consist of similar transfers for merchant seamen and the transport of prisoners of war from their camps to the various docks, where they were employed in loading and unloading vessels.

The various armed services provided 'fuel vouchers' for the supply of both petrol or diesel, which were similar to petrol coupons but listed the number of gallons authorised. For any civilian use a form had to be submitted to the Regional Transport Commissioner, listing every journey, with the mileage, undertaken, This form was called "Z': with a number, but after 60 years the number eludes me! Provided the journeys were accepted as essential (and I never knew them to be queried) fuel vouchers were supplied.

As the threat of u-boat activity in the North Atlantic decreased, there was some limited private hire allowed for civilian use. There was a limit of 50 miles from starting point to finishing point, but I cannot remember the exact radius. I am sure the files from the Ministry of War Transport would give more details. However, whatever the radius, we could get to Blackpool, Morecambe, and Helsby Hill (a children's pleasure park) amongst the local attractions. All these journeys had to be listed on the 'Z': form and the fuel was so authorised.

Liverpool Corporation did not have private hire powers outside of its own operating area, but ran in the operating areas of Birkenhead and Wallasey Corporations, technically 'on hire' to those operators on leaving the Mersey Tunnel. Likewise a reciprocal arrangement applied to them when operating in Liverpool. Journeys operating farther afield were 'on hire' to Crosville for those commencing in the south or centre of the city, to Thomas Lawrenson Ltd (then a noted coach operator) for the north end, Bootle and Litherland. There was so much work around at this time that when hires were booked, no reference was made to the firm concerned, but a docket sent to them after the operation, giving the price of the hires and the ten-percent commission they could bill for. Any other private operators were treated in a similar manner, if they introduced work. This produced difficulties when at one time the Ministry declared that the fuel used on these hires had to come out of the allocation of the 'official operator' – and this put a stop to such hires for a time, though the ruling was subsequently rescinded. From about 1948 all this was relaxed and normal hiring and fuel arrangements took over.

# HISTORY IN THE MAKING?

It is often the case that one encounters in looking at old newspaper files some bus reference, the background to which is not readily apparent, you only have to look at some of the queries that arisen in these Newsletters over the years. Michael Dobbs reports a more recent (2001) case in his home town that may well be mulled over half a century hence. Spilsby, Lincolnshire, had a humble bus shelter located in the High Street, the pre-cast concrete variety with a wooden bench along the back, glass at the front and one entrance. With the development of the high profile *Interconnect* network in the county it was proposed to upgrade this with one incorporating real-time information facilities, etc. The Spilsby Town Council came out against, it was 'too modem and not in keeping with the town' (pre-cast concrete was?) but the Town Mayor was to be castigated for later speaking in favour. Apparently it was a case of having the shelter, work on which was in any case underway, or losing the chance of a grant for another one. Cue for a District Councilor to bring the issue to the fore, condemn the council for discussing the issue 'in committee' and for passing a letter around a meeting that he had asked to be read out! All headline news in the *Lincolnshire Standard*, naturally. One wonders if any of those involved had had occasion to stand in that bus shelter on a cold winter's day, wondering if the bus will arrive, and, if so, whether they then spent the time fruitfully considering the architectural merits of the concrete in relation to the surrounding buildings Somehow one doubts it.

# EARLY SCOTTISH BUS HISTORY

*In N/L 100 Tony Newman submitted the following report and correctly posed the point that perhaps we somewhat neglected Scotland. A response quickly followed.*

From time to time there are comments made that the history of bus services in Scotland are neglected. There are some obvious exceptions, one or two dedicated researchers have done some excellent work. As a spur to encourage further study of services on Lewis, the following clues are drawn from an Appeal hearing of 1947. The full transcription of the shorthand record of the proceedings has survived in file MT33/244 at the Public Record Office.

The appeal marks what was probably a last battle between the pre-war contestants for the rights to run certain bus services on the island. The contestants were John McIver, trading as Back Motor Transport (becoming an incorporated Limited Company on May 15, 1947) of 24 Lewis Street, Stornaway, and John Mitchell of 37 Matheson Street, Stornaway. The contested decision of the Traffic Commissioners was published in N&P 288 of 5 July, 1947. The file contains a timetable and fare-table for the service from Back to Stornaway.

One of the underlying factors in the dispute was the problem of getting the (drunken) customers away from the pubs in Stornaway, without leaving the more sober cinema patrons stranded. The pubs closed at 9pm and the Chief Constable wished to get the inebriated back to their villages as quickly as possible, the cinema peformances seldom ended before 10.30pm. How were these two needs for transport to be met?

In weighing up the arguments to resolve this question a considerable amount of historical information is recited and recorded in the evidence. It appears that as at September 1939 there were no less than 63 operators of road passenger transport on Lewis. This was an abnormally large number of operators for a comparatively small area. Each operator was said to be a dual-purpose carrier and when the passenger vehicle was not engaged in the business of carrying passengers it was utilised for goods. The buses were a very mixed collection of vehicles, with seating capacities varying from 7-20. By 1947 the buses were larger, mostly seating between 20-32.

The transcript also contains details of the dates when some of the services to Stornaway were begun. George Stewart began a service in 1924, and was soon to be followed by John Murray in 1925. In May 1942 John Murray was joined by his brother Angus and they traded as 'J & A Murray' on the Back service. John McIver began his service from Coll the same year. In 1937 there was an operator running a service from Tong to Stornaway but this ceased when fuel rationing began. John Mitchell had began his service from Tolsta in about 1938 and early in the war he had acquired the businesses of three small operators operating in Coll, Gress and North Tolsta. During the war there was some sharing of operations on a rota basis.

This is a bare outline from which further study might begin to build up a fuller account of the buses operated on the Isle of Lewis. (AGN)

## EARLY SCOTTISH BUS HISTORY – ISLE OF LEWIS (RESPONSE BY RICHARD GADSBY)

I was extremely interested in Tony Newman's article in N/L 100 covering a snap shot of early bus services in Lewis, not least the reference to the record of the proceedings which survived at the Public Record Office – this is something I will follow up. As one with a keen interest in the early Scottish bus scene, I thought it would be appropriate to follow up Tony's excellent article, with a hope that we can help to achieve Tony's objectives further with research into ' a fuller account of the buses operated on the Isle of Lewis.'

Starting with reference to George Stewart and John Murray pioneering services from Back to Stornoway in 1924 and 1925 respectively, there were some other pioneers in different parts of the Island worth mentioning. W. Smith, of Borve, pioneered a service from Barvas (in the north-west) into Stornoway soon after the Great War, using a wartime Ford T ambulance, which was adapted to a 14-seat bus by Smith. Brothers Donald and Neil Finlayson commenced a service from their home base in Skigersta (in the extreme north) to Stornoway in about 1921, and operated this continuously for 28 years, until this was sold to John Mitchell of Stornoway, mentioned in Tony's article.

John MacLean of Aird (on the west coast) started a service from his home base to Stornoway in January 1924. Finally, Norman Murray of Habost (again in the extreme north of the Island) operated from Ness to Stornoway from 1925. Murray was also a merchant and lemonade manufacturer, and his son, Donald, also operated over this route from 1927, using an Overland vehicle. Most of the many operators would have had another line of business, such as Murray, the passenger operation being an extra small income to their livelihood Unusually, Murray's Overland (JS 2904) had a proper bus body, rather than the usual, typically rather basic, use of a goods vehicle fitted with some form of seating Reference was made in Tony's article to 'dual purpose' vehicles. These were usually licensed as ' Goods and Hackney' (see N/L 101-ED) (or equivalent), and such vehicles usually seated between 5 and 14. Life in the mid-1920's on the Isle of Lewis was such that the only means of transportation from those outlying villages into Stornoway – the main market centre and fishing port of the Island, was through these vehicles, and it made obvious sense to combine goods and passengers transportation.

Stewart's first identified 'bus' was a 1927 Ford T (JS 2999) which was a goods vehicle, with facility to carry 8 passengers, and Murray's first vehicle was a brown 1925 Ford TT (JS 2479), which was licensed for goods and 14 passengers. These vehicles were typical of the period, and a high percentage of all new vehicles purchased on the Island at the time were Fords, with Chevrolet coming a strong second By the 1930s, the picture had changed to Bedford being the dominant marque, with Commer vehicles (via a local dealer Henderson Brothers in Stornoway) next numerically. Most, but not all, of the vehicles were based on goods chassis, whether or not they were fitted with true bus bodies.

Two local bus body builders have been identified – Duncan MacDonald, of Cross, and John MacLeod, of Port of Ness – both of whom built many bodies for vehicles in both the Isle of Lewis and the Isle of Harris. There was also a coach builder, Norman Campbell of Port of Ness, who converted buses into lorries, which reflects the fluid nature of the operations at the time, with many changes of ' licensing' arrangements (e.g 'Hackney/Goods' to Goods only' or whatever.)

Many of the Bedfords came new via John Mitchell, who as well as being an operator, was a Bedford dealer. Mitchell started stage-carriage services in June 1932, and operated six of their own buses during the late 1930s mainly Bedfords, but with some Albions on goods chassis. Trading as 'Mitchell's Transport Parcel Service', the title clearly reflects the dual role of operators at the time. Sporting a light and royal blue livery, Mitchell continued to expand – being registered as John Mitchell (Stornoway) Ltd after the war – and using a fleet of the inevitable Bedfords, until they ceased trading in 1980 – services then being taken over by various local operators.

To complement Tony's remarks regarding the 1947 licensing issue, we have a story that in September 1938, Mitchell commenced two services from Stornoway to North Tolsta, and to Portnaguran – Traffic Commissioners stating that some of the other competing operators should specialise in either passenger or goods services, and not both, as many were doing at this time. Tony mentions 63 operators in September 1939 – but to give an even bigger picture of the chaos at the time, some 171 licensed operators plied for trade at some time between 1930 and 1940, admittedly throughout the Outer Hebrides (including Isle of Harris and Isle of Uist). How they all made ends meet given the nature of the services provided is an interesting question!

The merging of Murray and Stewart (and also John MacIver of Back) into Back Motor Transport Limited in 1947, was part of a wider rationalisation of companies into bigger groups taking place around this time, and which helped to reduce the number of competing operators serving the outlying districts to and from Stornoway. For the record, the following additional take-overs took place during the early Post War years:-

By October 1946, HEBRIDEAN TRANSPORT Ltd, Stornoway took over Angus Campbell, Portnaguran; John M. Campbell, Portnaguran; Donald W. MacDonald, Garrabost; Donald MacLeod, Portnaguran; John MacLeod, Porvoller, Alexander MacMillan, Lower Grarrabost

By January 1949, GALSON-STORNOWAY M.S Ltd, Lower Barvas took over Malcolm MacKenzie, Barvas; Malcolm Morrison, Barvas; Morrison & MacDonald, Barvas; Malcolm Smith, Lower Barvas

By January 1949, WESTERN LEWIS COACHES Ltd, Stornoway took over John McArthur, Breasclete; Peter MacAulay, Carloway; Murdo MacLean, New Shawbost; Alexander MacLeod, Barvas; A.W. MacLeod, South Bragar, J.A. MacPhail, New Shawbost

In addition, Mitchell took over Evander MacIver, North Tolsta; Donald MacKenzie, Portnaguran; Donald MacLeod, Luerbost, all in 1947 – as well as Finlayson, already mentioned. Thus the chaos that had ruled the Isle of Lewis bus scene had been stabilised by 1950, and only two one-man businesses were plying for passenger trade by 1961 – these being those of John MacMillan, of Lemreway, and J.M. Morrison, of Gravir, who shared a service from Lemreway to Stornoway on alternative dates.

So ended a very colourful period of competitive bus activity on the Isle of Lewis, which in most other parts of Britain had been stabilised much earlier, by the early to mid-1930s in most cases. There are still many gaps in the full story, however, and I would be delighted to communicate with anyone interested, or who has knowledge of, the early Scottish transport scene – not just in the Outer Hebrides.

*Overleaf are some evocative Isle of Lewis scenes from the Roy Marshall collection, Omnibus Society Photo Archive*

MacMillan
Bedford OB;
note the lack of
side mouldings,
see page 51.

Albion of
Hebridean
Transport.

Galson-
Stornoway M.S
with local
bodywork.

(All from Roy
Marshall
Collection, OS
Photo Archive)

# PLYMOUTH JOINT SERVICES – A DIFFICULT BIRTH
## BY ROGER GRIMLEY (N/L 132, 2008)

*The situation of Plymouth where two rivers, the Plym and the Tamar, flow into the fine natural harbour of Plymouth Sound gave the city great strategic importance during the Second World War. The Dockyard was the major employer of civilians in the city and there were Naval, Royal Marine and Army Barracks, a Flying Boat Station and many defence installations in the area bordering Plymouth Sound. This made it a target for German bombers and resulted in what became known as the Blitz. Over four years 5,000 properties were destroyed, 1,174 people were killed and a further 1,000 seriously injured in raids on the city.*

Plymouth Corporation Transport ran bus services and one remaining tram route in the city area, half the fleet being needed for works journeys. Western National ran inter-urban routes and served the growing suburbs that became part of the city in 1938. The municipal operator thought that it should have the right to serve the latter and relations between the two were very strained.

As the raids continued people sought safety in the surrounding countryside and the population of the city dropped from 220,00 to 127,000. Every evening there was a mass exodus from the city with people crowding on to the buses and trains, lorries being commandeered to take even more. This still left substantial numbers and columns of people walked out to the rural areas every evening searching for somewhere to stay in relatively safety-barns and even hedges providing some sort of shelter. Scenes like this are now seen on television during emergencies round the world. At the height of the blitz collapsed buildings and unexploded bombs caused considerable disruption and the "bush telegraph" was used to pass round changes in routes and stopping places. Following the destruction of the main shopping centre, travel patterns changed as an area a mile or so north of the centre became the main district.

On a Western National route restricted to single-deckers due to low bridges, perimeter seating allowed extra standing room. Travelling in a tightly packed bus with masked interior lights one had to be alert as it took time to get to the back in readiness for your stop and Conductresses had to show considerable ingenuity to pass through the bus collecting fares and punching tickets in semi darkness. This route passed the depot and those already seated dreaded seeing a bus waiting outside as this inevitably meant a change of vehicle. They could only watch in horror and dismay as the standees raced to the other bus and gratefully took all the seats. Another hazard was air raids while travelling and passengers were quickly ushered to the nearest air raid shelter.

Workers were brought to Devonport from a wide area with special journeys leaving Torquay (35 miles), Ashburton (25 miles) and Kingsbridge (25 miles) at around 5am. Dockyard workers whose houses had been destroyed were housed in temporary accommodation at Lee Mill, near Ivybridge from where two or three double-decker loads travelled daily. Already overcrowded Western National routes were placed under even greater strain and the situation was exacerbated when both operators' depots received direct hits destroying facilities and vehicles. Western National sought help from the Corporation but their request for vehicles was refused on the grounds that buses bought with public money could not be used for private profit. The use of fuel facilities was also denied until an influential Council member intervened.

Even though the company was permitted to increase peak-hour services, provided mileage was saved elsewhere, there were many complaints about the situation. On longer routes the bus would draw in and the conductress would announce that the first stop would be at a point well out into the country leaving those on shorter journeys to join a long queue for another route. Seeing an opportunity to achieve a long held ambition the Corporation sought permission to run to a number of places outside the city. This was fiercely resisted and at the prompting of the Regional Commissioner the two parties began discussions. However, these came to nothing and the Corporation again sought to expand into the suburbs outside the city bringing predictable protests from the company who argued that if more facilities were required they should provide them. The

Regional Commissioner, irritated by the stream of complaints and the apparent inability of the two operators to get together, became more forceful and this led to another round of negotiations.

After much detailed and often fractious discussion it was agreed to set up Plymouth Joint Services with an 80%/20% split in favour of the Corporation. Also written into the agreement was a condition that the company would not increase the proportion of double-deckers operated at 30 September 1939 of one to 2.362 single-deckers, without specific agreement.

The new arrangements came into effect on 10th January 1943, some company routes being extended across the city centre and the Corporation buses finally reaching places outside the boundary. In spite of some early problems things settled down and within a couple of years those who had expressed bitter opposition were admitting that there had been many benefits. The co-operation continued for many years until political ideals led to renewed competition. But that is another story!

**PHRG**

# FORCES' COACH SERVICE DISASTER SILVER STAR MOTOR SERVICES ACCIDENT 30 APRIL 1956

## REPORT FROM TONY NEWMAN

*Further to the talk given by Andrew Waller, at the 2006 Annual Meeting Birmingam, on the subject of Forces' Leave Services from Salisbury Plain, the Ministry of Transport Report on an accident in 1956 may be of interest. The Report describes a number of features that were part of the regular operation of these services.*

HWV 793, a 1952 Leyland Royal Tiger Coach, No.13 in the fleet of Silver Star Motor Services of Porton Down, Wiltshire was allocated to the service from Porton Camp to Newcastle-upon-Tyne over the last week-end April 1956. The service had been running since November 1955. It was scheduled to set out from Porton at 15.30 on Friday 27th and reach Marlborough Crescent Bus Station, Newcastle the next morning at 05.45. A period of 14 hours 15 minutes was allowed for the journey of 316 miles, which included 30-minute breaks at both Leicester and Leeds. On this particular trip, the relief driver was not picked up at Burford as planned, and the original driver was faced with a difficult decision. Rather than disappoint his passengers by spending time trying to contact his colleague, he opted to continue on his own. Indeed, it appears that he made every effort to shorten the journey and drove faster than he should, in order to give the service personnel more time to enjoy their leave, in Newcastle.

Once arrived at the destination, the driver chose not to take up the accommodation available to him and got what sleep he could on the back seat of his coach. He was scheduled to begin the return journey at 17.30 on Sunday 29th and to travel via Durham, Darlington, Boroughbridge, Leeds, Doncaster, Mansfield, Nottingham, Leicester, Rugby, Banbury, Burford and Bulford. Once again, the driver drove faster than he should and was stopped by the police somewhere along the route for speeding, but allowed to continue.

During the night the coach was travelling along the B4100 and at about 02.40 near to Birdingbury Wharf, it left the road, hit a tree and suffered considerable damage. Six of the passengers were killed and eight more were injured. At that date, the B4100 was closely on the alignment of the present A426. Birdingbury Wharf is not at the village of that name, but where the road crosses the Grand Union Canal, close by the Boat Inn. Although there are suggestions in the Report that the driver used unauthorised roads on the journey, it seems likely that the B4100 was part of the

**The ill-fated Royal Tiger No 13. (OS Photo Archive)**

authorised route. In the course of the enquiry into the accident, some of the passengers suggested that the driver had been hit on the head by luggage falling from the rack. The investigators did not accept this, but concluded that the driver (Reginald Bowley, aged 27) had become exhausted and had fallen asleep at the wheel. His PSV Licence was revoked, but the police did not press charges against him, nor against the owners of the coach.

The foregoing is a summary of what the Official Report tells us. We may still speculate on some aspects of the unfortunate story. Was the driver right to continue on his own? I have discussed the case with Derek Giles, who is of the opinion that this driver's hours at the wheel were just within the law in 1956. In those days, drivers' hours were not to exceed 11 hours in any 24-hour period, calculated from 2am. The Statutory Rest Period was 10 hours in 24. Of course, how the driver spent the rest period could not be controlled, but provided he was not driving a vehicle, the law was satisfied. What about the speed of the coach? The schedule of 13 hours 45 minutes (after deduction of the break times) for 316 miles requires an average speed of 23.8 mph. What we do not know is whether the coach left Newcastle on time or whether its departure was delayed waiting for latecomers.

They were due back at Porton Down at 07.45, just in time for the 08.00 expiry of the service men's leave passes. There is no suggestion that the coach was travelling excessively fast at the time of the accident, but the possible lack of sleep and strain of keeping to time may have caused the driver considerable tiredness. The Report does record the fact that the driver had four previous convictions for speeding.

The coach was recovered from the site after the accident (but only after a press photograph was taken by Hamblin) and its Leyland body was replaced with a Harrington body in July 1956. It was also renumbered from 'unlucky' 13 to 28, and passed to Wilts and Dorset in 1963. A copy of the Report may be seen at The National Archives under File Reference MT102/115.

# LETTER FROM DEREK GILES

*"In his interesting article in N/L 137 (The Glasgow Coaching Ventures of Cameron & Cambell, three parts, 135-137 ed) Richard mentions that Lowland Motorways operated a number of stage services to new housing estates in the east end of Glasgow after the second World war. This prompts me to raise a question which has puzzled me for the past fifty years. How did Lowland obtain licences for those services, which it seemed to me were in good bus territory and well patronised? One might expect GCT and/or SMT to strongly resist invasion by another bus operator. Did they object? Did staff shortage discourage additional commitments? Was H C H Moller (md and guiding light of Lowland) on good terms with SMT?"*

The letter from Derek Giles (NL138) regarding Lowland Motorways caused much interest amongst the Scottish fraternity of Allan Condie, George Heaney and Iain MacGregor, and a number of e-mails flowed around on this topic. The following summarises the situation well, and comes courtesy of Ian MacLean whom Iain contacted for his thoughts on the Lowland question:

"In the early 1950s, Lowland had a successful summer coach business, but needed stage carriage routes for balance. At this time Glasgow Corporation had made a start on building the new Cranhill housing estate, about four miles east of the city centre, and one mile north of Shettleston, which was almost a self-contained community, with a good shopping centre, cinemas, public houses, schools and churches.

It was not Glasgow's policy to include such amenities in new housing areas, and as all the Transport Department's and Scottish Bus Group's bus routes were east-west, the new residents would be faced with long journeys to Glasgow's East End for necessities and comforts. Lowland knew that they would prefer to travel to Shettleston, and that the Transport Department was unable at that time to provide vehicles or staff for new services, and so would be unlikely to oppose new routes in areas it did not already serve.

Black's Taxis' (H.R. Black of Springboig) main route was north-south from Macnair Street in Shettleston to Queenslie Industrial Estate, on the opposite side of Stepps Road from Cranhill, and was the key to opening up the area. So Lowland purchased the business (in April 1952) and transferred the licences, thus becoming the existing operator. Taking the long view, routes were then set up along new roads with minimal initial housing, thereby making Lowland almost fireproof from objections in Traffic Courts.

A Craven bodied RT of Lowland.

From memory, those objections which were offered were from Glasgow Corporation Housing Department and Lanarkshire County Council, on the grounds of suitability of roads which had not yet been upgraded.

One objection from Lanarkshire was on a Lowland application to run double-deckers via Gartocher Road, where the railway overbridge was stated on Ministry of Transport records to have a clearance of 13ft 10in; Lanarkshire maintained the clearance was 13ft 9in., while a board on the site indicated 14ft. The proposed double-deckers were 13ft 6 in., and the application was approved after a site visit!"

*Richard Gadsby*

## An appeal, not exactly unknown from Editors, from 2005
# QUESTIONS & ANSWERS

Or perhaps a dearth of same recently. One of the features of this Newsletter, certainly its strength, since inception has been the great diversity of both the queries raised by group members and (more often than not) the answers that are provided We have ranged from pointing out previously recorded facts, the whys and wherefores of various regulations, personalities, as well as background information on specific operators. Obscurity has certainly been a continuing theme, but so also has come enlightenment.

Thus it is with regret that one has to admit to a distinct drying up of this to and fro between group members, at least via this N/L, in recent months. It is difficult to believe that we have -managed to achieve nirvana and answered every query that was and so the appeal is made to bring forward any items to which you have either searched in vain for or which have long puzzled. This applies particularly to our more recent recruits, if indeed our longer term doyens have now exhausted their stock of questions.

# MISCELLANY, THE ODD THINGS RESEARCH FINDS

**Fishy Business:** During the General Strike in May 1926, Provincial Tramways Co Ltd of Grimsby had fourteen vehicles, including a number of coaches and buses, delivering fish to all parts of England, journeys up to 600 miles being undertaken. Nearly 150 tons of fish was transported during the strike and over 17,000 miles covered. Reaction of passengers when the vehicles returned to ordinary service (*"Conductor, there is a funny smell on this bus..."*) is not recorded. *(Commercial Motor Archive)*

**Customer Care:** an interesting view of the needs of actual or potential passengers was expressed by Adrew Nance, the forthright manager of Belfast City Tramways who, in 1914, replying to a questionnaire upon night services – (not provided in Belfast) – said *"We absolutely decline to issue a schedule to the public"* and further *"In Great Britain and Ireland running a tramway service between midnight and 7am is simply playing the fool. It only serves to prevent the sleep of sensible people"*. (unknown source, from Derek Giles)

**It takes All Sorts:** Seventy-five of the ugliest people in London travelled to Herne Bay by motor-coach. They were members of the Society of Natures Misfits. Their President said that he is the ugliest diamond broker in Europe. Because he found his unprepossessing looks a social handicap he formed the society for 'social self protection'. The society has amongst its members six of the ugliest members of the Stock Exchange, an ugly comedian and a soap manufacturer. *"We spend every weekend together, any member taking steps to make him self good looking is expelled. We search London to find the ugliest motor-coach drivers to take us away at weekends,"* says the president. *(Booking Agents Journal, Sept, 1930)*

**Trump this:** Miss S... Summonsed before Camberwell Magistrates for refusal to pay the hansom cab fare demanded, protested that the cab horse had been 'unpleasantly flatulent' throughout the journey and the driver most uncouth when remonstrated with. Having (one can imagine) some difficulty in controlling the proceedings, the Bench ruled the driver could not be held responsible for the 'natural functions' of the animal (but might attend its diet better) and the case was found proved, with costs. *(Cab Trade Gazette, 1901)*

# SOUTHDOWN 'CHASERS'

## BY ALAN LAMBERT
### Article originally published in Newsletter 134, 2008

*In common wan most large bus firms Southdown generally accepted that small operators who had been the first on a road should be left alone. Where, however, an operator started up in competition on what they considered was their territory then it was a different matter.*

During the 1920s several operators sprang up often using small 14-seat vehicles on pneumatic tyres, which were permitted to run at 20mph. Southdown's lumbering Tilling-Stevens and Leyland buses on solid tyres, which were restricted to 12mph, were obviously no match.

Consequently in October 1926 an order was placed with Dennis for eighteen 30-cwt chassis to be fitted with Short Brothers aluminium bodies fitted with 19 seats, which had an unladen weight of less than 2-tons so that they could run at 20mph. A nineteenth Dennis was fitted with a Harrington body incorporating Weymann fabric patents. In order to maintain the benefits of the faster speed it was decided to employ 'boy-conductors' of 14-years years of age which was permissible on vehicles with less than 20-seats – and at lower rates of pay. Unusually for such small vehicles they were all fitted with rear-entrances although this was standard Southdown practice on their larger vehicles. They were delivered between March and June 1927.

However, after the order had been placed, Southdown took over the two operators running on Hayling Island. Holt's Motor Services ran from Rowlands Castle to Hayling and Stride between Hayling and Havant. With Stride's business came a Morris 18-

seat bus which was under 2-tons and was thus considered to be part of the 'chaser' fleet making the total twenty.

Southdown quickly re-organised the routes so that service 48 ran from Waterlooville to

Courtesy Alan Lambert collection.

Courtesy Alan Lambert collection.

Hayling and service 49 from Horndean to Hayling via Rowlands Castle. Each route ran two-hourly giving an hourly service between Havant and Hayling. Because of the weight-limit on the bridge to Hayling Island, small vehicles were required for these routes and a Vulcan joined the Morris.

The first two new Dennis buses thus found themselves allocated to these routes and when the frequency was increased in May 1927 by an additional hourly Havant-Hayling journey they were joined by a third Dennis, although this was not the role for which they had originally been intended.

In Portsmouth, Southdown had continuously been at loggerheads with Portsmouth Corporation over fares within the City and was obliged to charge higher fares to protect the tramways. However, by some curious anomaly the Southsea Tourist Co. did not have this restriction and after Southdown took that concern over in 1925, the public started to complain about being charged differing fares on different Southdown buses for the same journey.

In July 1925 Portsmouth Corporation extended their Southsea-Copnor-Cosham service to Drayton and charged a lower fare than Southdown over the Cosham Drayton section. The Corporation were entitled to do this as Drayton was the city boundary, but Southdown had always considered this 'road' to be their territory. In retaliation, Southdown started charging the lower fares on all their routes within the city and forced the Corporation into discussions over the whole matter.

This proved to be very protracted and it was not until July 1927 that an agreement was made that the Corporation would withdraw their Drayton route and Southdown would charge protective fares on all their routes within the city. To replace the Corporation buses a new 'fast' service 43 was introduced running every 15 minutes from Drayton to Southsea. This did not run to a timetable, except from the terminals and took five of the little Dennis buses. Two other Dennis' were being used on service 12D. This never appeared in any timetable, although there is a passing reference to a service operating to Denton in 1928/9 official documents so presumably this was it.

So, it was only in Eastbourne that these buses were used for their real purpose. The competition that Southdown suffered from E.E. Piper and H. Twine in the Eastbourne area has already been described in newsletter 114 and it is not perhaps surprising that five of these vehicles (including the Morris) were used in that area. From June 1927 this number increased as services 91 and 92 were completely operated by these buses. They were also used on additional short workings on services 12 and 25 that could not be fitted into the normal schedules and on an un-numbered service to Wannock operated in competition with Twine.

Three other Dennis' were used on rural services where the patronage was very low. Two were used on service 81, which linked Haywards Heath with Billingshurst and one was used on a new service 82 from Haywards Heath to Horsham.

In the summer of 1928 the route from Hayling to Havant was extended to Portsmouth and the resident buses transferred thereto. There they remained until 1931 when some new light-weight Tilling-Stevens buses arrived to replace them.

In December 1928 Twine, who was already in competition with Southdown between Polegate and Eastbourne, extended his route to Alfriston. This clearly upset Southdown who put two chasers in front of his buses between Polegate and Eastbourne. Twine then complained to the Chief Constable of Eastbourne about Southdown's tactics. Eventually they came to an agreement that Twine would with-draw from Alfriston and Southdown would withdraw the 'chasers' and not run to Wannock or Jevington. Not surprisingly, Twine also started negotiations to sell the business to Southdown, which took effect in September 1929. Piper had already succumbed in April and at this point the Dennis' days as 'chasers' were over.

A few were used on rural routes and one was also used to run to Peacehaven Annexe when that route started in September 1929. An increase in the speed limit of all buses on pneumatic tyres to 20mph in October 1928 also helped to seal their fate.

Most were withdrawn in 1931 (the Morris having only lasted to the end of 1927) although a few struggled on for another year. It is interesting to note that although the idea was sound at the time, it was quickly overtaken by events, including the Road Traffic Act 1930 which put a stop to such tactics.

# A SERIAL COMPETITOR?
# – ERNEST EDWIN PIPER
## N/L 112, 2004, FROM ALAN LAMBERT

*One of the fascinating things about research is finding the unexpected. The story starts with research in the Guildford Watch Committee Minutes where it was found that one E.E. Piper of High Street, Ripley, Surrey applied for a licence on 29 December 1924 to run from Ripley to Guildford via Ockham, Horsley, West Horsley. East and West Clandon and Merrow.*

On 14 January 1925 his vehicle PA 6716 (make unknown) was presented for inspection. It actually failed, requiring two fire extinguishers, a bell and cord plus a wooden partition to separate the driver from the passengers. From the registration number this bus would appear to be nearly ten years old, so whether Piper had used it on routes elsewhere or recently acquired it to start this route are matters of conjecture. This bus was licensed again in June 1925 at Guildford.

When buses were required for inspection again in June 1926 we find that the route is now in the names of Piper & Chell and PE 1666 and PE 5941 were presented for inspection. When a new bus PF 4732 was presented for inspection on 5 October 1926 it was in the name of Leslie Steele Chell. Bridge Road, Ockham only – Piper having departed. Chell subsequently sold the business to East Surrey in January 1928, moving to Eastbourne and setting up Glideway Coaches, running an express service between there and London. (See account in N/L 104). Piper obviously departed from the partnership soon after June 1926 for on 9 September he registered his first bus in East Sussex, an Overland (PM 7058) from Knights Farm, Hellingly, trading as Red Saloon Motor Service.

His first route was from the Golden Cross Inn to Eastbourne via Hailsham and Stone Cross, but here he was in conflict with the Southdown service 29 between Golden Cross and Hailsham, but wisely avoided the direct route via Willingdon where Southdown were already in conflict with Henry Twine. With the arrival of two more buses, in the spring of 1927, he increased the frequency of the Eastbourne service and started a new one from Hailsham to !Pevensey Bay via Polegate and Stone Cross. He also erected a garage at Lower Dicker, said to have been in use at the old Airship station at Polegate.

This move coincided with the arrival of the first of Southdown's Dennis 30cwt 'chasers' in March1927 and several of these were put on service 29 to generally 'harass' Mr Piper. In June 1927 service 29 was renumbered 92 and the 16 from

Brighton to Golden Cross was extended to Eastbourne via Stone Cross on a two-hourly frequency, thus increasing the competition. This situation continued largely unchanged until March 1929 when both 92 and 16 started running via Stone Cross, making for an hourly frequency. At this point Piper decided he had had enough and approached Southdown to take over his business, which they did from 10 April. He then moved to Devizes.

The Red Saloon fleet and staff during the Eastbourne period, it must be assumed that Ernest Piper is the non-uniformed figure on the right. (Courtesy Alan Lambert collection.)

Thanks to Roger Grimley we now know what happened next. 'He was in business at premises on the Bath Road He chose a good place in which to compete with Western National, for the area around Devizes is where the territories of Bath Tramways Motor Co, Wilts & Dorset and the National met and relations between them were highly sensitive. Each needed to be very careful not to appear to invade the others space and in addition to the three combine Companies, the then still independent but relatively large Lavington & Devizes Motor Services were involved.

Still trading as Red Saloon Motor Services he exploited this to the full, starting services in the Devizes, Melksham and Trowbridge area, then cutting prices and adopting 'pirate' tactics when National responded. He caused them a great deal of trouble until eventually on 1 June 1931 they acquired his business. The routes operated appear to have been: Trowbridge – Seend – Devizes; Trowbridge – Holt – Melksham – Melksham Forest; Melksham Forest – Melksham – Atworth.'

More information can now be added. Ernest Piper was born 1900 and served briefly at the end of WW1 in the London Regiment, a territorial battalion. The family home was the Knight's Farm at Hellingly where he returned to after the Guildford period. He had married in 1922 and Leslie Steele Chell was his brother-in-law. By 1939 he had settled at Hailsham as an automobile and electrical dealer, a business that continued post-war. He died in 1975.

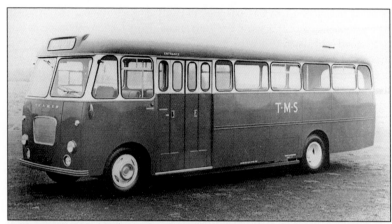

Amongst the few early bus bodied Ford Thames 570E was a batch bodied by Duple for Trimdon Motor Services that featured a unique double door width. (Duple photo courtesy Philip Kirk)

Delivered to Kemp, Margate, from dealer stock in July, 1965, FAP 360 C was possibly the last 570E to be registered. Seen in May, 1971, it already represented a fast disappearing breed. (photo copyright Brian Weeden)

# HOW FORD ENTERED THE MARKET PLACE

## THE THAMES 570E REMEMBERED BY DAVE BUBIER

*By 2010 and N/L 145 the range of our research articles was broad and included, as here, some vehicular matters. Your Editor makes no apology with completing this anthology with one of his own contributions as it touched on some little understood issues that had led to misnomers and needed a clarified record.*

Although the ubiquitous Model T had figured in some numbers in the fleets of small embryo operators post WW1, the Ford motor company in Britain never pursued the passenger vehicle market with specific models to the extent of their competitors. Only limited numbers of subsequent goods models were so bodied over the years. It therefore came as something of a surprise to the industry when, in May 1957, the introduction of the new Thames 'Trader' 7-ton goods range was accompanied by an announcement of a corresponding passenger chassis aimed at the lightweight sector of the market. Powered by an entirely new 5.4 Litre 6-cylinder front-mounted diesel coupled to a four-speed box, the prototype was bodied by Duple with a version of their 'Vega' 41-seat body and weighed in at 5 ton 2¼cwt. A petrol version was always available but, so far as is known, never taken up.

Whilst doing the demonstration rounds various necessary modifications were identified, particularly to the springing. This particular vehicle was later (November 1959) to figure in a 45-hour non-stop trial run to Moscow organised by Vernon Maitland of Excelsior, Bournemouth. The poor roads encountered revealed rather more deficiencies in the bodywork than the chassis! A couple of pre-production models were supplied to selected operators and a Burlingham 'Seagull' bodied example for Ivory Coaches of Tetbury made a first appearance for the make at the 1959 Brighton Rally. Initially designated the Thames 510E in accordance with Ford practice of their commercial range bearing that name, the refined production version became the 570E.

Bedford had dominated the lightweight sector in the mid-1950s, only Commer coming close and with Austin having bowed out without ever offering a model to the 30 foot (41-seat) dimensions. Petrol was still widely favoured in the private sector, although the 1956 Suez crisis had hastened the move towards diesel. Commer had already switched to their 3-cylinder horizontally opposed TS3 (nb, it was never a 'two-stroke' the TS stood for Tilling-Stevens!), which had its devotees but certainly divided opinion. Bedford only offered the proprietary diesel option, Perkins R6, which was not universally loved, but was .slowly developing its own unit. It was an opportune moment for a newcomer as the huge post-war intake of coaches was

The BET Group ordered a goodly number of Duple 'Yeoman' bodied 570E for allocation to subsidiaries for private hire and excursion work, mainly in single numbers but Timpson and, as seen here, Yorkshire Woollen District took batches. (UK Bus Archive)

rapidly becoming time expired and demand growing to update to the now 41-seat 'norm', leading to a buoyant second-hand market. Additionally many who had previously favoured 'heavy-weight' models were now looking closely at the cost benefits that lighter models might offer in enabling more frequent fleet updates.

The 1958 Commercial Motor Show saw the more formal launch of the 570E, alongside the Bedford 300 cubic inch diesel version of their SB range (SB1), with substantial orders being taken for 1959/60 delivery. Rather than leave sales entirely with their main dealers, who had little experience of the trade in second-hand coaches, Ford enabled a number of smaller specialist dealers to pre-order batches of complete vehicles for resale. It was an astute move that undoubtedly assisted the rapid establishment of the 570E as all but the market leader for the ensuing years. Main bodybuilders were Duple (who branded as 'Yeoman' a version of their 'Super Vega' model and Burlingham with the stylish 'Seagull 60' but which proved a problematic design, leading to their collapse and takeover by Duple. Plaxton, Harrington and Thurgood also bodied the 570E, unsurprisingly as it differed little from that intended for the Bedford. Primarily the 570E was coach bodied but there were a small number of service buses, notably a batch for Trimdon Motor Services. The BET Group tried a Harrington bodied example with East Kent (which was subjected to merciless treatment!), then ordered a significant quantity with Duple bodies for successive year deliveries to a number of subsidiaries, including Timpson, YWD, Stratford Blue, etc.

The relative merits of the Thames 570E against its Bedford SB1 counterpart provoked much discussion but in truth the differences were not great. The price of the 570E was pitched a little lower than the Bedford – in November 1958 it was quoted as £1,175 and complete with Duple body at £3,735. Some preferred the more upright driving position compared with the Bedford raked steering wheel, which had the best ride was argued. Most conceded the 570E was more capable of a severe 'thrash'. This last was a consideration as the motorway network grew and the limitations on end-to-end cooling patterns emerged. Both manufacturers hastened to refine their engines by 1962. The new Ford version had a marginally better BHP and was higher revving than the new Bedford 330 but this maintained at 28mpg – an edge over the 570E at 26. Air-over-servo brakes were introduced and five speed boxes the norm rather than an option. Battle for supremacy in the lightweight market did see one casualty at this time. Commer, unable to further develop the TS3 to accommodate larger vehicles, withdrew from the passenger market after 1962.

The increase in maximum length for PSVs to 36 feet led to a dilemma for the lightweight manufacturers. Bedford decided to adopt the radical design of the six-wheel VAL using a larger Leyland engine. Ford managed to retain a four-wheel layout using the existing drive train mounted ahead of the front wheels and designated 676E. Bodied by Duple as the 'Marauder' (later 'Mariner') and also, surprisingly, by Harrington from 1963 it was beset with teething problems and attracted few buyers. It was soon superseded by the development of a new model utilising an upright version of the new engine developed for the Thames 'Trader' replacement, D series but it was well into 1965 before full production of this new R series, in two wheelbase lengths, got underway. Henceforth the branding was as 'Ford', the 'Thames' one dropped. Production of the 570E had ceased in 1963 but residual chassis were bodied in the 1964 and 1965 seasons, possibly the last to be registered entering service in July 1965. Bedford, with their strong non-psv and overseas market were able to continue the SB model for many more years to come.

The Thames 570, whilst having only the briefest of production runs from 1959 to 1963, had nonetheless a profound impact on the market during that time. Sadly it was to disappear after a relatively short period. By the early 1970s the 41-seat front-engine coach was decidedly 'old hat' but whereas plenty of Bedford SB were to be found in the lower echelon fleets the earlier 570E was not so common and by the end of that decade any found were a considerable rarity. One factor determining this rapid demise was that Ford always geared their spare parts availability to goods vehicle life spans whereas Bedford were far more in tune with the extended life times of their passenger models. Even when the first 570Es came up for their renewal COF in 1965/66 it was reported minor problems arose in this respect and all the evidence is that this became ever more acute once the model was long since deleted from the catalogue. For all these reasons the Thames 570E did not even loom large in the 'hippy' convoys of the 1990s and only a very few found favour within the preservation movement.

# A FORMIDABLE LADY

## BY JOHN DUNABIN – (N/L 85, 1999)

*We finish our trawl of the first 25-years of PHRG material with a piece that has previously been reproduced but which is so much the essence of the whimsical style of the author as to deserve a permanent record. Mrs Meredith (nee Baynham) dates are 1892-1974 so this interview was from the early 1970s.*

When years ago my interest in road passenger transport crystallized into a study of its history, an unexpected bonus was discovering the pleasure of listening to some of the pioneers, rugged pioneers, with their families and early employees. Most of them struggled hard to recall everything about their careers, and I never once encountered a complete refusal to talk.

Some few I was very loath to approach, knowing something of their reputations, but in one instance my hand was forced. The person in question was a lady renowned for her sharpness of tongue and her business toughness; although there were two of her brothers in the business everybody knew who was boss. She was widowed fairly early in her marriage, with one son who had been groomed to take over the business who also died quite young. Her future must have looked bleak, and I decided to leave one possible source of Herefordshire bus history untapped.

However I was blessed – the word is carefully chosen – with a former school friend who was a teacher, a much loved one too, in the local grammar school which her son Derry had attended. This without any special contriving provided our entree, and we were both invited to tea with the 80 year old lady, an opportunity too good to refuse.

The occasion was a very civilised one, even cosy, a plate on ones knees, thin cut fresh salmon (Wye salmon, or course!) sandwiches, with plenty of hot tea served in lovely china. To begin with I was sitting on the edge of my chair minding my p's and q's, but the atmosphere was reassuring and I even accepted without demur a very disparaging view of my near vintage classic car parked outside.

I cannot remember now if the reminiscences began before the last crumb was consumed and the last cup of tea drunk, but I don't think I could have attended to the latter as the stories came tumbling out, all delivered with a self parodying twinkle but with a twist like a Saki story or an Oscar Wylde fairytale.

First came a straightforward account of the start of the business by her father,

George Baynham Snr carrying mails, etc, from Mitcheldean on the edge of the Forest of Dean of Dean. The next step took him to Ross on Wye, a much larger town and a growing tourist centre at the time, where after a number of moves the business became established in the Swan Hotel yard. Conveyances, all horse drawn, were provided for local journeys, meeting trains (Ross was then served by rail), but one of the drivers at least had to stay close at hand. Part of the business included providing horsepower for the town fire engine, and the young Miss Baynham's job, on hearing the fire alarm, was to head for the Swan yard and have the horses ready and hitched up before firemen arrived. That on one occasion her keenness to reach the fire she spilled some of the firemen off came as no surprise to her audience, but then came the first sting in the her tale; she told us of her father being too drunk to find his way home and having to rely on the horses to do so.

Facts came tumbling out in plenty, such as the fitting of gasbags to the now motorised taxi-cab fleet in WWI, with a bill for £125 when Miss B unthinkingly drove under a canopy at Ross railway station. The canopy has long since vanished, as has the station itself. The first and only motor charabanc owned by Mr Baynham was described as a Milnes-Daimler Mercedes. Under his daughter's management, adding to Delauney, Belleville, Studebaker and less exotic sounding makes of car, came two Palladium 'charas', a Garford, Fords, a Guy, and at least two, probably three Chevrolet. Prices for the latter ranged from £465 to £495. Having purchased the first of them in London Miss Baynham was so impressed with its running by the time of reaching Reading that she decided to buy another. It was not made clear whether she turned back there and then!

In around 1923 the business was experiencing competition in the charabanc excursion field from a company based likewise originally at Mitcheldean, which had taken over part of the Royal Hotel garage in Ross (occupied at one tune by the Baynhams). Miss Baynham's solution was to buy into the new company, becoming one of its directors, but this did not prevent her from accusing one of her fellow directors of arson when the Mitcheldean garage burned down.

Many years later and for similar reasons, in this case warding off possible competition, a smaller local business was acquired. Miss Baynham, by now Mrs Meredith*, had not until then had any experience of running local bus services, not wanting as she put it, to be tied down (the Mitcheldean business stopped running buses after that fire!), but on the latter occasion there was no easy way out and when

---

EDITOR'S NOTE: *Miss Victoria Irene Baynham married Harold Meredith, a Bridstow farmer, in 1920, separately continuing the garage business she had inherited from her father, who had died in 1914.

told of the takings on their newly acquired stage services by the bus driver and former owner she felt strongly that she was being cheated. But apart from suspected untrustworthiness on the part of her business associates, some customers aroused her ire.

One ostensibly potential customer was different. Persuaded by somebody to advertise an excursion not included on her wide ranging licence, she was approached by a seemingly casual enquirer. Equivocating, her cautious reply was to say that she had not made her mind up, suggesting he should call again. He never did. Not long afterwards, appearing before the Traffic Commissioner she recognised the Chairman, Col. A.S. Redman as her enquirer. He recognised her too, of course and leaned over to ask: *"Did you ever run that tour?"* I don't know what answer she gave, nor if she ever did!

Most of the anecdotes though concerned cab and not charabanc passengers. This could have arisen because of Miss Baynham, being in a position to choose, undertaking the more private work. On the other hand it could relate social attitudes of 80 years ago. 'Charas' were for large parties of the less affluent, who could and did get drunk on their seaside jaunts, but rarely displayed the eccentricity, a euphemism for ill-mannered arrogance, often shown by their 'betters'. Here I am tempted to move beyond the normal boundaries of transport studies or rather bus enthusiasm; perceived social class governs decisions as to whether to use the motor bus now more than it ever did!

Charabancs in general catered for 'ordinary' people who did not have their own transport, offering affordable days out for those who could not afford to develop or at least not to display any eccentricity. Cabs, Victorias, etc, (Miss B had one or more of the latter) were for the more affluent who for one reason or another did not have their own transport available, but felt obliged to make clear that they were really 'carriage folk'. The fact remains that the elderly Mrs Meredith uttered no criticism of her many charabanc customers, some of whom must have been offensive at times, but looked on some of her taxi-cab passengers with a very critical eye.

Two remembered passengers who provoked no adverse comment were the noted actor/playwright Seymour Hicks and his wife Ellaline Terris, well known as an actress in her own right, who were visiting Goodrich Court for the fishing. Arriving, Hicks thought it too cold for fishing, hid behind a tree and persuaded their driver to take him back to the station. Less welcome was a novelist/writer who got her drivers drunk, including her son Derry who had an accident as a result. The natural solution for somebody of Mrs Meredith's temperament, was to decline his further custom.

In general the stories were of occasions where the teller had come off best, but one did not fall into this category. A local lady insisted that she must not be looked at, at all by her driver on her journeys, and always took several minutes to 'compose' herself before alighting. Starting off was even touchier, the technique being to wait for the click of the door before drawing away. Once Miss Baynham was quite sure she had heard that click and set off on a seven-mile journey. Reaching her intended destination, after a customary wait she had heard nothing and risked a peep only to find she had no passenger! The only conclusion was that the latter must have fallen out, so the worried driver retraced her route, slowly and looking hard. At her starting point again, there was the intended passenger, ready with brandy for Miss Baynham in case she was suffering from shock!

Another story, told without hint of apology, showed the raconteur, seemingly now so full of good humour, in a less favourable light; not for nothing was she sometimes known in Ross as 'the old trout' , a change from 'Rene the Swan'! Collecting a lady and her daughter from Ross station she learned that they had been to the opera, and remarked that she too liked opera, particularly 'Carmen'. The response from the lady which would have riled most people, was that she thought opera would have been over her (Miss B's) head. The reaction was prompt and considerable. The cab was a Ford Model T with trembler ignition, so a quick hand movement under the dash could simulate failure. The ladies alighted to climb the hill, while the supposedly stranded driver headed for home. Not one to do things by halves, when she saw another of her taxis about to pass her she flagged the driver down and warned him not to give the involuntary pedestrians a lift. The trembler trick also came in handy when a male passenger made what used to be described as unwelcome advances. He was left with an eight mile walk!

There should be some sort of epilogue to this story, or perhaps another more pungent anecdote. Mr W.E. Morgan (Wye Valley Motors) to whom Mrs Meredith ultimately sold the business after her son Derry's death, was well known for his tough, even savage, business tactics, but she was uncharacteristically reticent about their negotiations. Perhaps I met her too soon after the event, or possibly they were too painful to recall.

# FINIS

# JOHN E. DUNABIN
# 1916-2002

Co-founder, Chairman and major contributor to the formative years of our
Group was particularly known for his interests in the bus services of
Herefordshire. An evocative Chas Klapper view of Hereford Bus Station.
© OS Photo Archive

# LIFE IN SPACE

## David Glover

Heinemann Educational Publishers
Halley Court, Jordan Hill, Oxford OX2 8EJ
a division of Reed Educational & Professional Publishing Limited
www.heinemann.co.uk

Heinemann is a registered trademark of Reed Educational & Professional
Publishing Limited

First published 2000
Original edition © David Glover 1998
Literacy World Satellites edition © David Glover 2000
Additional writing for Satellites edition by Christine Butterworth

04 03 02
10 9 8 7 6 5 4 3 2

ISBN 0 435 11930 3   *LW Satellites: Life in Space* single copy

ISBN 0 435 11934 6   *LW Satellites: Life in Space* 6 copy pack

**Illustrations**
Julian Baker, title page, pages 8, 15 and 19. Joe Lawrence, contents page and page
21 bottom. Oxford Illustrators, pages 5 and 18. Arcana, page 11. Maltings Partnership,
page 21 top.

**Photos**
Photo Library International / Science Photo Library, page 5. Science Museum / Science
and Society Picture Library, page 6. NASA, pages 9, 10, 16 and 17 bottom. Genesis
Space Photo Library, pages 12 and 17 top. NASA / Science Photo Library, page 13.

Designed by M2
Printed and bound in the UK

**Also available at Stage 2 of *Literacy World Satellites***

ISBN 0 435 11933 8   *LW Satellites: Natural Record Breakers* single copy
ISBN 0 435 11937 0   *LW Satellites: Natural Record Breakers* 6 copy pack

ISBN 0 435 11932 X   *LW Satellites: The Roman Chronicle* single copy
ISBN 0 435 11936 2   *LW Satellites: The Roman Chronicle* 6 copy pack

ISBN 0 435 11931 1   *LW Satellites: Have Your Say* single copy
ISBN 0 435 11935 4   *LW Satellites: Have Your Say* 6 copy pack

ISBN 0 435 11939 7   *LW Satellites: Teacher's Guide Stage 2*
ISBN 0 435 11938 9   *LW Satellites: Guided Reading Cards Stage 2*

# CONTENTS

# WHAT IS SPACE?

When we look at the stars, we are looking into space.
Space is the name for everything beyond our Earth.

## What is in space?

Our Earth floats in space. Beyond Earth there are planets,
stars, moons and comets. Some of these are much bigger
than Earth. They look tiny to us because they are so far away.

The whole of space is called the universe.

## The Sun

The Sun is the star that is closest to Earth. It is special for
us because it gives us the heat and light we need to live.

The Earth goes round the Sun in a circle. This is called the
Earth's **orbit.** The Earth takes a year to do one orbit of
the Sun.

## The Moon

The Moon is a ball of rock in orbit round the Earth. Each Moon
orbit takes one month.

## The Solar System

The Sun and its nine planets are called the Solar System.

Planet Earth is made of:

- rocks
- liquids (such as water)
- gases (such as air).

There is a layer of gas and air around Earth. This is called the atmosphere. The atmosphere gets thinner as it gets further away from Earth.

A diagram to show where Earth is in the Solar System.

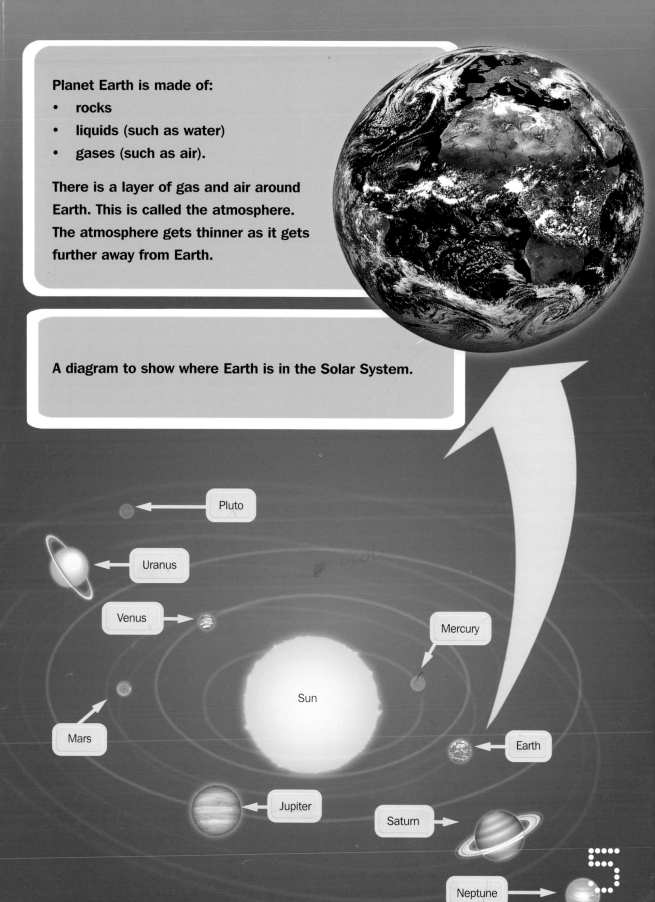

Pluto

Uranus

Venus

Mercury

Sun

Mars

Earth

Jupiter

Saturn

Neptune

# WHY DO PEOPLE EXPLORE SPACE?

People have always wanted to know more about stars and planets. What are they made from? How far away are they? Can we go to them?

## Looking into space

**Astronomers** are people who study space. They watch stars and planets through telescopes, and work out how far away they are.

Astronomers have worked out that a jet plane would take 20 years to reach the Sun. But it would take half a million years to get to the next nearest star!

Galileo was the first astronomer to look at the Moon through a telescope.

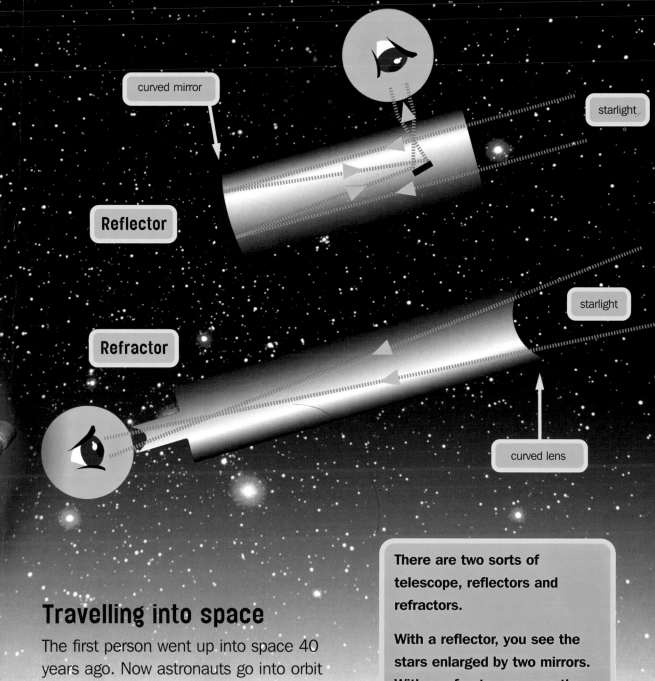

curved mirror

starlight

Reflector

starlight

Refractor

curved lens

# Travelling into space

The first person went up into space 40 years ago. Now astronauts go into orbit round the Earth to do experiments. They also test and mend equipment.

One day, people may go to live on the Moon and other planets.

There are two sorts of telescope, reflectors and refractors.

With a reflector, you see the stars enlarged by two mirrors. With a refractor, you see the stars enlarged through a curved lens.

# HOW DO SPACECRAFT TAKE OFF AND LAND?

Astronauts travel into space inside spacecraft.
The spacecraft is powered by **rockets**.

A Russian SL-4 rocket taking off. Three astronauts sit in a module near the top. There is not much for them to do. Take off is controlled by computer.

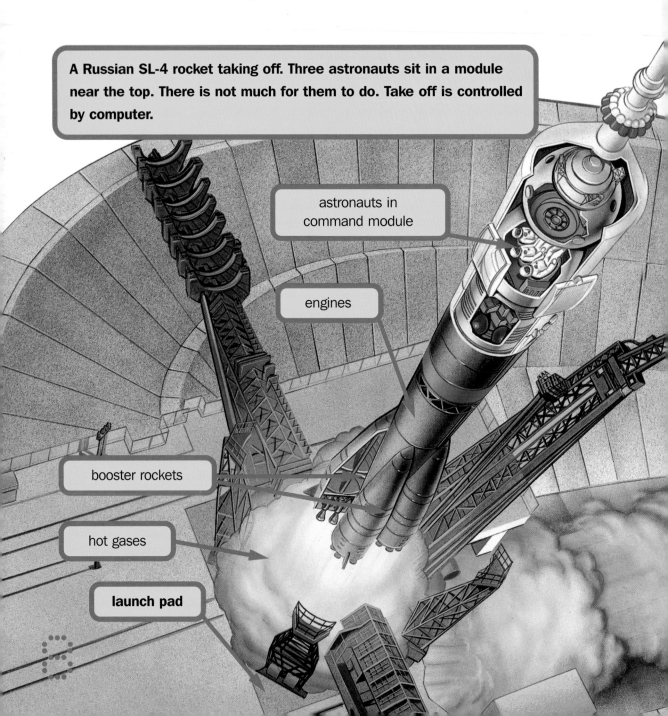

astronauts in command module

engines

booster rockets

hot gases

**launch pad**

## Taking off

When the spacecraft is ready to take off, hot gases shoot down from the rocket engines. Their force pushes the rocket up into the air.

**Booster rockets** add more power. The rocket needs a lot of power to get away from Earth's **gravity**.

The engines turn off when the craft is in orbit. A spacecraft does not need engines to move in space.

## Landing

When the astronauts want to come back to Earth, they start the engines again. The engines push the spacecraft out of orbit, and gravity pulls it back to Earth.

Then the spacecraft lands in the sea, or on a runway.

**A space shuttle landing on Earth.**

**A parachute helps to slow it down.**

9

# WHO CAN BE AN ASTRONAUT?

Many people want to be astronauts, but only a few are chosen.

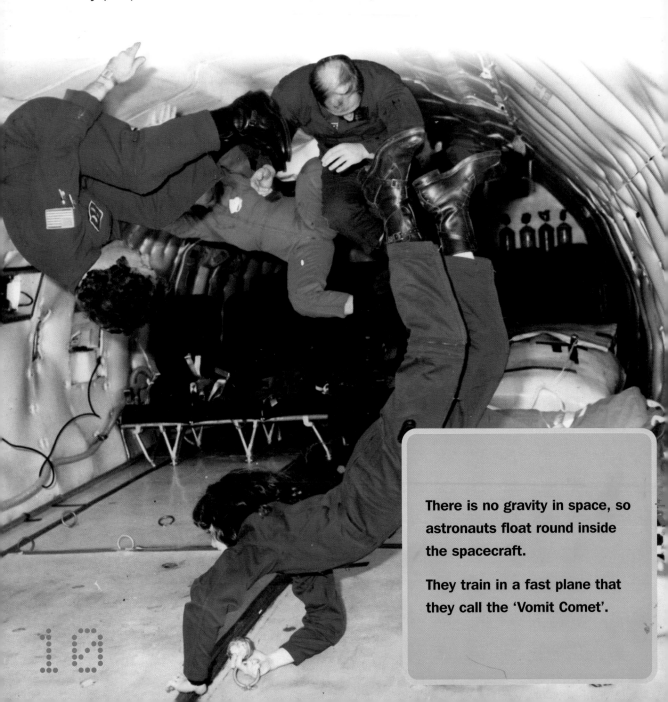

There is no gravity in space, so astronauts float round inside the spacecraft.

They train in a fast plane that they call the 'Vomit Comet'.

# Astronauts at work

There are two kinds of astronaut.

## 1. Space pilots

Space pilots fly spacecraft.

Spacecraft are much harder to fly than planes, so space pilots must already be able to fly jet planes.

## 2. Mission specialists

These are scientists who do experiments and look after the equipment.

They all have their own special jobs on the mission.

# Good astronauts

Astronauts must be fit. They need strong bodies to stand up to the forces when a **rocket** takes off.

They also have to be good at living together and getting on with each other.

This is a training wheel for astronauts. It helps them get used to spinning and turning, as they will in space.

# WHAT DO ASTRONAUTS DO?

Astronauts do many different jobs.

They mend old **satellites** and launch new ones.
They build **space stations** and do science experiments.

## Science in space

Space is a good place for experiments. Because everything is weightless, things act differently. For example, chemicals mix together better. This is because one chemical is not heavier than another.

In the future, there may be factories on space stations for this kind of work.

**These tomatoes were grown on board a spacecraft.**

**In the future, astronauts on long journeys will need to grow their own food.**

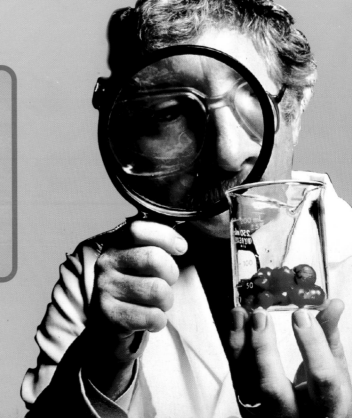

# HOW DOES A SPACESUIT WORK?

An astronaut needs a **spacesuit** to go outside the spacecraft.

There is no air in space, so the spacesuit and helmet give the astronaut air. The life support system on the back keeps the air fresh.

On Earth the suit would be too heavy to wear. But in space everything floats, so the weight is not a problem.

## Staying safe

The suit is made of many layers of special cloth. Dust specks travel through space at thousands of miles an hour. The layers of cloth protect the astronaut from the dust.

## Staying cool

The underwear has tubes of water running through it to keep the astronaut cool. The helmet has a visor to keep out the strong sunlight.

## Staying in touch

Inside the helmet, the astronaut wears a cap with a radio in it. The radio links with the spacecraft.

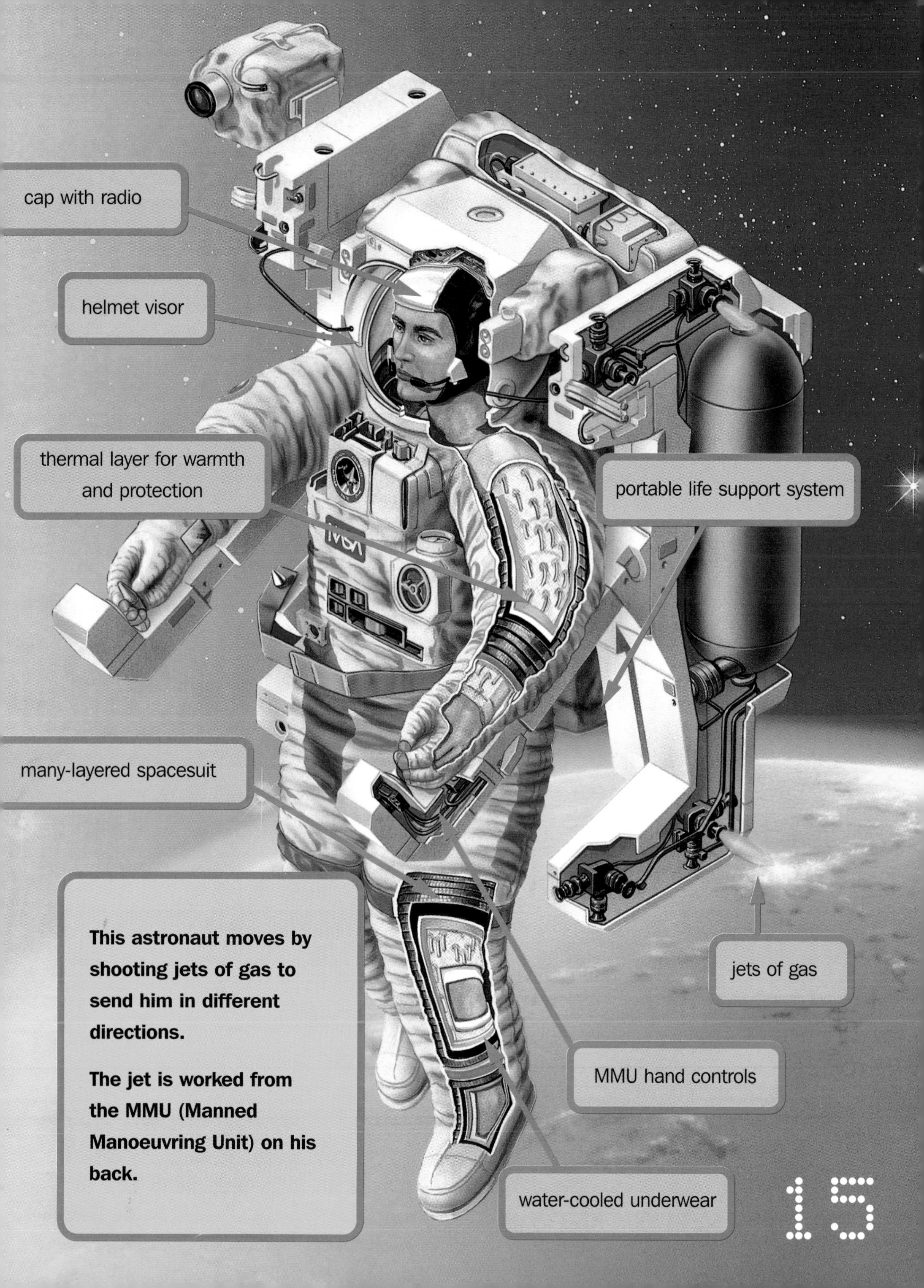

cap with radio

helmet visor

thermal layer for warmth and protection

portable life support system

many-layered spacesuit

This astronaut moves by shooting jets of gas to send him in different directions.

The jet is worked from the MMU (Manned Manoeuvring Unit) on his back.

jets of gas

MMU hand controls

water-cooled underwear

15

# HOW DO ASTRONAUTS LIVE IN SPACE?

Life in space can be tricky. Without **gravity** everything floats about. Special containers are used to keep things in place.

## Space toilets

Going to the toilet could be messy because there is no gravity to make the waste drop into a toilet bowl. Space toilets solve this problem.

They work like a vacuum cleaner, and suck away the waste. The suction is strong – sometimes the astronaut gets stuck to the seat!

## Keeping fit

Astronauts float everywhere, so they hardly use their muscles. They must exercise to keep their muscles strong.

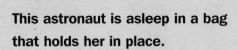

SLEEP RESTRAINT

**This astronaut is asleep in a bag that holds her in place.**

**Astronauts can fall asleep in any position – they don't need to lie down!**

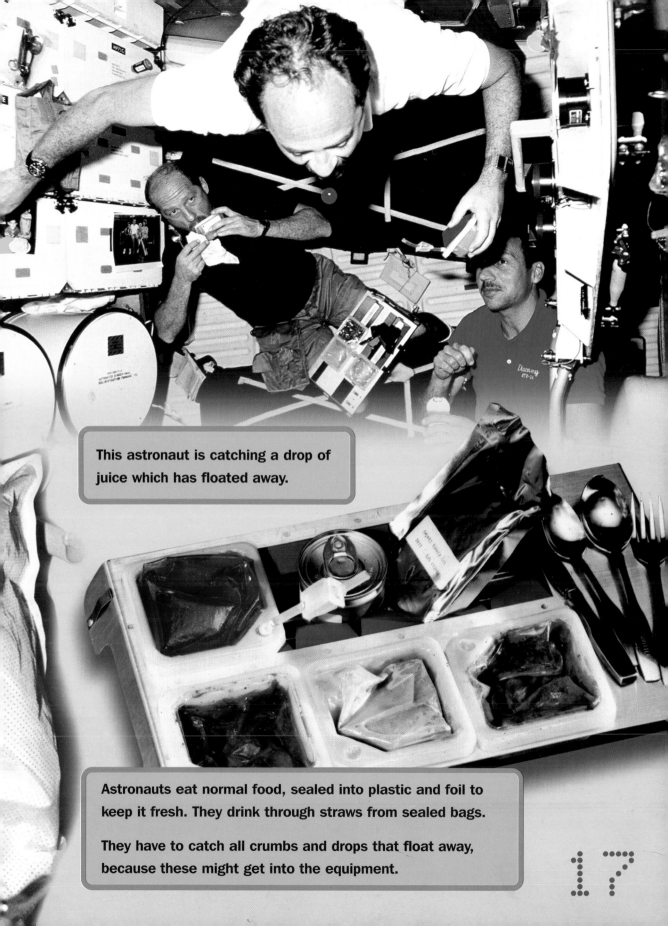

This astronaut is catching a drop of juice which has floated away.

Astronauts eat normal food, sealed into plastic and foil to keep it fresh. They drink through straws from sealed bags.

They have to catch all crumbs and drops that float away, because these might get into the equipment.

# HOW IS A SPACE STATION BUILT?

A **space station** is like a house or an office in space. It stays in **orbit**. Astronauts live and work in a space station, doing experiments and testing equipment.

## Building a space station

A space station is too big to be taken up all at once by **rocket**. It is made up of parts called modules.

Modules are taken up one at a time, then joined together in orbit.

A module is taken up in a space shuttle. It will be joined to other modules by round doors called ports.

Joining on the module is called **docking**. Once it has docked, the inside doors open and astronauts can move from one part to another.

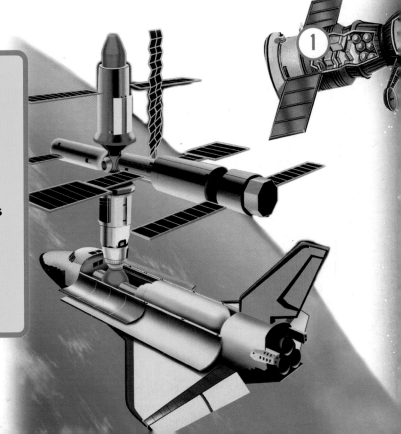

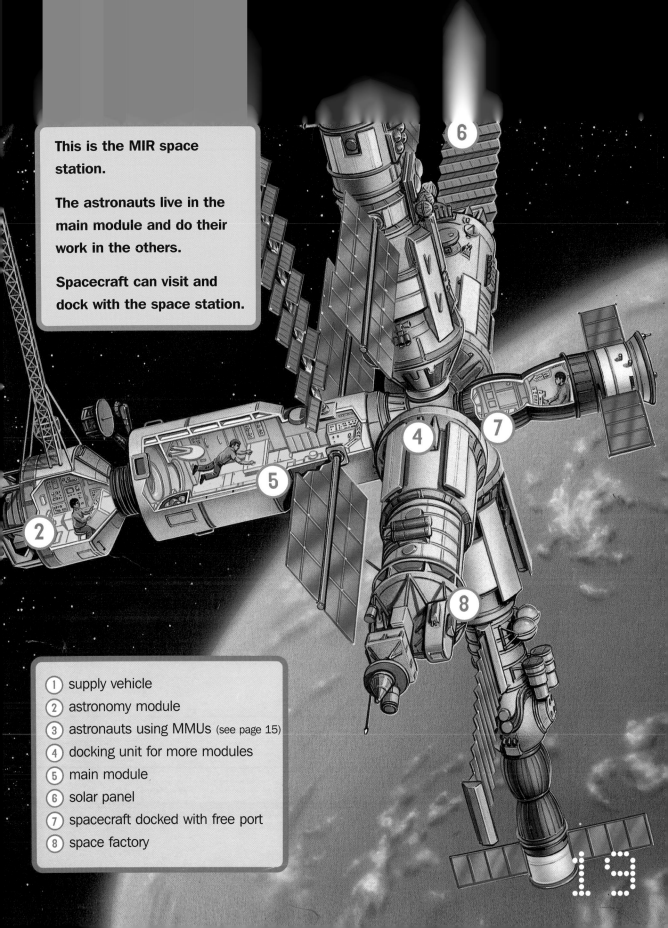

This is the MIR space station.

The astronauts live in the main module and do their work in the others.

Spacecraft can visit and dock with the space station.

1. supply vehicle
2. astronomy module
3. astronauts using MMUs (see page 15)
4. docking unit for more modules
5. main module
6. solar panel
7. spacecraft docked with free port
8. space factory

19

# WHAT IS A SPACE PROBE?

A **space probe** is a craft sent far out into the solar system.

It does not carry astronauts. Its job is to send back information about the planets.

## How far can a space probe go?

Space probes have been to most of the planets in the solar system.

In 1997 America sent a probe called Pathfinder to land on Mars.

Pathfinder used huge airbags to soften its landing.

After it landed, the air was let out of the bags.

The robot on the left is studying a rock.

28

Voyager was a 'fly-by' probe.

In the 1980s it flew by Jupiter, Saturn, Uranus and Neptune and sent pictures back to Earth.

Now it is heading for the stars.

The Mars Observer was an 'orbiter' probe. It was sent to orbit Mars in 1993.

After a while it broke down, and it no longer sends back signals.

# Into the future

Probes tell us about planets that astronauts may go to in the future. In 2011, America plans to send a team of astronauts to Mars. Maybe in the future we will all be able to visit the planets!

# SPACE TIMETABLE

| | mission | purpose |
|---|---|---|
| 1957 | Sputnik 1 | First satellite in orbit |
| 1957 | Sputnik 2 | First animal in orbit (a dog called Laika) |
| 1961 | Vostok 1 | First person in orbit (Yuri Gagarin) |
| 1969 | Apollo 11 | First landing on the Moon |
| 1973 | Skylab | First space station |
| 1976 | Vikings 1 and 2 | Robot landers on Mars |
| 1981 | Columbia | First space shuttle |
| 1981 | Voyager 2 | Robot space probe passes Saturn |
| 1986 | MIR | Space station built from modules |
| 1993 | Mars Observer | Space probe sent to orbit Mars |
| 1997 | Pathfinder | Robot lander on Mars |

# GLOSSARY

**astronomer**
a scientist who studies the stars and planets

**booster rocket**
a small rocket linked to a bigger rocket to give extra power at take off

**docking**
joining two spacecraft or parts of a space station

**gravity**
a force which pulls things towards the Earth

**launch pad**
the flat area from which a rocket is launched into space

**orbit**
when a satellite (or moon, or spacecraft) circles around a star or planet

**rocket**
a tube filled with fuel that burns to push a spacecraft into space

**satellite**
an object such as a spacecraft that is in orbit around a planet

**shuttle**
a spacecraft which can take off, orbit the Earth, land, and be used again

**space probe**
a robot spacecraft sent to explore other planets

**space station**
a home and workplace built in space

**spacesuit**
the special suit with a helmet that astronauts must wear in space

# INDEX